Abuse of Trust

Abuse of Trust: A Report on Ralph Nader's Network

Capital Legal Foundation

REGNERY GATEWAY
CHICAGO

Published by Regnery Gateway
360 West Superior Street
Chicago, Illinois 60610

Library of Congress Catalog Card Number: 81-85566
ISBN: 0-89526-661-X

Contents

Introduction

My first impressions of Ralph Nader were formed during the "anti-establishment" days of the 1960s, when I was a student in college and law school. In those halcyon days of youth, the name Nader evoked the image of a diminutive, courageous private citizen, without money, connections or old school ties, who dared to battle the industrial megaliths of Detroit and Houston and the political lobbies in Washington. I shared his avowed goal of making consumer products safer. I believed—as I still believe today—that this was a laudable, desirable, and attainable goal.

First impressions fade more slowly than others. What I read of Mr. Nader in subsequent years raised little doubt in my mind about the value of his activities in American society. I now realize, however, that I did not scrutinize Mr. Nader and his associated organizations carefully enough to recognize that my impressions were wrong. It is a failing that remains prevalent to this day among the public in general, and the media in particular.

I took my first hard look at Mr. Nader's activities after I became president of the Capital Legal Foundation in May of 1980. Capital is a non-profit, tax-exempt public interest legal foundation based in Washington, D.C. Its primary concern is federal regulation of economic activity. The foundation maintains a free-market economic philosophy, a healthy distrust of all large institutions—including government—and a pronounced concern for the poor and working classes of the United States.

Although I had previously practiced law in large and small firms and had spent some time in the federal government, my knowledge of the public interest law movement was scant. Naturally, after joining the foundation, I decided to learn more about the movement promptly. Ralph Nader's groups seemed the obvious place to start.

As part of this educational process, I turned to a summer intern at Capital, who had just completed her junior year at Yale, and asked her to prepare a researched memorandum on the legal positions, operations, and extent of Mr. Nader's groups. After several weeks of research, she reported that relatively little information was available. There were numerous newspaper and magazine articles that quoted or named Mr. Nader and his attendant organizations, and there were one or two poorly documented books written by his former associates—now old friends or new enemies. But this was not the kind of thorough information that you would expect to find about one of the most talked about, if not influential, popular movements and personalities of the 1960s and 1970s. Anyone like Ralph Nader, who had rested long in the public eye, organized sizable groups, and acquired immense public prestige, should have already undergone intensive scrutiny by the press and other independent observers. So I sent the intern back to the stacks.

In an attempt to supplement her library research,

the intern requested information directly from various Nader-related organizations. They were generally unresponsive, evasive and at times hostile. Repeated searches of public records, which are normally a cornucopia of incisive facts and figures, yielded nothing new or little of substance. Copies of publicly available tax records were similarly uninformative.

At this point, I felt torn about the Nader project. On the one hand, it was becoming obvious to me that his organizations were probably larger, wealthier, and more numerous than had been publicized. It was even clearer that these groups had quite deliberately erected a citadel of silence around their operations. The uniformity with which they closed ranks whenever we made inquiries led me to think of a homogeneous grouping that was fearful of outside intrusion. Mr. Nader, it became apparent, had produced a tightly knit network of vested-interest lobbies rather than a vast number of unrelated groups addressing issues in the public interest.

On the other hand, I foresaw no worthwhile purpose in attempting to breach those ramparts of silence. There was no clear evidence at that time that Mr. Nader or his groups were reprehensibly disingenuous. I was willing to retreat from the citadel of silence. I accepted it as an unfortunate—albeit understandable—paranoic response to the so-called persecution that Mr. Nader claimed to have suffered at the hands of his opponents in the mid-sixties.

However, before we stopped our inquiries, we decided to try one last source, in this case the District of Columbia Department of Licenses. Any organization that solicits funds from the public in the District must file annual information reports with the department in order to qualify legally as a charitable group. To our complete astonishment, the Office of Licenses and Permits advised us that the Nader organizations we inquired about had *never* filed any information returns or any exemption requests with the District. Furthermore, the head of the Investigation and Inspections Office for the department, Joseph Richards, asked us to file a complaint against the Nader groups to force them to comply with the law.

Failure to comply with any law is a serious matter, and failure to heed a law intended to shield the public from fraudulent solicitation is very serious indeed. Frankly, I found it incredible that the Nader groups would disregard any law, let alone one that required the kind of public disclosure that Mr. Nader had made a career of advocating for others. Moreover, I knew that the District of Columbia's charitable solicitation law was not unique. This type of law is common in this country—33 jurisdictions have ones like it—and it is well known to tax-exempt organizations raising money from the public.

Here was evidence that a number of organizations run or directed by Ralph Nader for more than ten years had failed to comply with disclosure rules of the type he sought to impose on other groups in our society. What did this say about a man whose name had become synonymous with "open government"? What did this say about his incessant cries for more and more public disclosure from businesses and individuals? Why would he urge more government regulation of economic activity and fulminate against "crime in the suites," if his own groups failed to comply with existing law?

This discovery led me to suspect that the Nader network might be abusing the public's trust and that its secrecy or vagueness about its activities and finances

4

might be a screen to conceal the true nature of its conduct. I assigned two other interns, both of whom were law clerks, to assist in the investigation, and we began to dig hard for additional information about the Nader network.

Based upon Capital Legal Foundation's research, I now believe that much of what the Nader-controlled or -directed organizations do has very little in common with any of the public interest principles they seemingly avow to represent or protect. Our findings are set out in this book for the readers to judge for themselves whether the prevailing image of the Nader network is accurate. At the least, I hope this report stimulates discussion about the role of *all* the self-appointed tigers at the gates of the "public interest."

Dan M. Burt
Washington, D.C.
January, 1982

Chapter I
The Background

Ralph Nader's name has become synonymous with the consumer activist and "public interest" movements that have grown in prominence in the U.S. since the late 1960s. No other "public interest" advocate enjoys so much attention from the press, radio, and television, or is so widely known by the general public. No one else has so many direct links to the numerous consumer and "public interest" organizations throughout the country. And no one other than Mr. Nader is looked upon as the symbolic founding father of "public interest" activism.

In a relatively short period of time, "public interest" activities have had an immense impact on our daily lives. Through the congressional and federal regulatory processes, they have altered the contents of the food we eat and the drugs we consume; they have influenced the design of cars and appliances; they have helped change the way we finance election campaigns and made the governmental process more accessible to the public at large; they have influenced the style and content of advertising and even television programming; and they have taken a major part in the effort to clean up the environment.

Other advocacy groups have also utilized the "public interest" label to pursue more specific political agendas such as women's liberation, social services for the poor, gay rights, and anti-nuclear power. On the conservative side of the political spectrum, "public interest" groups have emerged to rally against bigger government, and to defend free enterprise and the rights of the individual against intrusion by the state.

"Public interest" advocacy has become one of the signs of our times. It embodies an inherent distrust of traditional political and social organizations to represent the public adequately and to wage the fight for the "common good." "Public interest" groups seek an alternative means of influencing decision-making in both government and industry. This most often takes the form of intervention in the regulatory processes of the federal, state, and local governments. Testimony is often given on behalf of the "public interest" before congressional committees and federal regulatory panels. In some cases, the groups elect to fight the issues out before the courts. Only in the Carter administration did the "public interest" movement gain sizable turf within the executive branch of the federal government. Joan Claybrook, a former associate of Mr. Nader, was a particularly notable example of this last because of her appointment as head of the National Highway Traffic Safety Administration.

Ralph Nader, more than anyone else, is responsible for the "success" of the "public interest" movement to date and for its ongoing vitality. His observations about politics, economics and society in the United States may often be wrong or ill-conceived, but it cannot be denied that Mr. Nader's activities still generate wide and, sometimes, intense interest from the general public, the media, and the decision-makers in Washington.

THE BEGINNINGS

In contrast to his current notoriety, Ralph Nader first came to public attention in a relatively small, albeit sensational, way. In 1965, he published a book, *Unsafe at Any Speed*, which criticized harshly the design and safety standards of car manufacturers.[1] He particularly criticized a General Motors Corp. car, the Corvair, which was later taken off the market (to the ire of Corvair enthusiasts, many of whom still maintain it was the best car they had ever owned).

Mr. Nader, who was an advisor to a Senate subcommittee that probed safety in the summer of 1965, also charged that automobile manufacturers subordinated safety to styling, speed, and horsepower. He said that the "safety establishment" was made up of industry-oriented organizations such as the National Safety Council and the American Automobile Association, which fostered the view that driver behavior, not design, was responsible for accidents.[2] The auto industry and AAA denied the charges, and some officials later questioned Mr. Nader's competence in auto engineering.[3]

Mr. Nader's book and his publicized remarks helped spark a *general* concern about automobile safety in America. He received even more public attention in March 1966, when he charged that he was "shadowed" by private detectives and harrassed by anonymous telephone calls because of his criticism of the car industry. Mr. Nader said he believed the auto industry sought to impugn his standing before Congress.[4] The manufacturers initially called the charges "ridiculous."[5] A couple of U.S. Senators promptly urged the U.S. Justice Department to investigate the charges.[6]

Within a few days, General Motors admitted conducting a "routine investigation" of Mr. Nader through a "reputable law firm." It denied any attempt at harrassment or intimidation, but said it sought to determine any link between Mr. Nader and parties in lawsuits against GM over the Corvair's design.[7] Mr. Nader denied representing any clients in the Corvair cases.[8]

In late March, GM President Roche appeared before a Senate subcommittee and apologized for the probe of Mr. Nader. Mr. Roche conceded that GM investigated Mr. Nader's personal affairs and that there was some harrassment, but he said that neither he nor any other executive knew of the investigation. Mr. Nader accepted the apology, but charged that GM sought to obtain "lurid data" for "invidious use."[9]

In November of 1966, Mr. Nader sued GM for $26 million for invasion of privacy.[10] Almost four years later, he got a $425,000 out-of-court settlement from GM. Mr. Nader pledged to use the proceeds to monitor GM's activities in safety, pollution, and consumer relations.[11]

THE NEXT STEP

With the help of the publicity from the GM affair, Mr. Nader amassed a wide public following and established several consumer and "public interest" groups, including Public Citizen, Inc., and the Center for the Study of Responsive Law. At the same time, his focus of attention spread beyond the automobile industry. Mr. Nader's concerns and those of his organizations expanded to include industrial accidents, misleading advertising, air pollution, airplane fares and safety, atomic energy, consumer credit, food additives, drugs, pesticides, railroad practices, and water pollution.

Underlying these specific concerns were two

main objectives: to make corporations more "accountable," especially through the use of government regulations, and "the reclaiming of government power by citizen power."[12] "The evils [in society]," Mr. Nader believes, "are an inevitable result of concentrated power that's insulated from broader human values."[13]

Eileen Shanahan of United Press International conducted a lengthy interview with Mr. Nader in January 1971, which revealed much about his thinking on governmental and corporate power, and the role of the citizen and "public interest" groups.[14] Asked if corporations and capitalism would exist in his "ideal world," Mr. Nader responded:

> I don't think we have a capitalistic system now. There are too many government controls over the market mechanism, too many subsidies and far too much oligopoly and shared monopoly over the market mechanism. It's much better, I think, to call it part capitalistic. The trend is to have increasing interwovenness between large corporations and large governmental units. This is why it's no longer a surprise for Penn Central [Railroad] to apply to Washington for welfare.
>
> We're heading into a greater and greater portion of the economy taking on the characterization of corporate socialism, which is basically corporate power utilizing government power to protect it from competition.

Nader cited as examples oil import quotas, large government subsidies, and the "socialization" of the risks and costs of corporate activities "through the tax mechanism or through inflated and constantly renegotiated contracts."[15]

However, Nader did not recommend less governmental intrusion in the private sector as a remedy. Instead, he called for *more* government involvement and the "popularization of the corporation."[16] One step, he said, would be the chartering of corporations by the federal government rather than the states. Such a federal charter would require greater public disclosure of information, including confidential tax statements, a consumer complaint procedure, a bill of rights for employees, greater shareholder involvement, less protection of "trade secrets" and national elections—or "popularization"—"for, say, five out of 20 directors" on a corporate board.[17] Mr. Nader also called for more accountability by company officers, who would be liable to suspension under law, and for possible suspension of advertising by companies that violated their federal charters.

In regard to the role of citizenship in the United States and Mr. Nader's own activities, he told Ms. Shanahan of UPI:

> I see myself working in the corporate regulatory arena to develop models, techniques, procedural advances that can be used by other groups that have their own interests to advance—whether it is in civil rights or electoral reform or what have you.
>
> The basic point, of course, is to develop what in ancient Athens was called the public citizen, with the main difference being that we don't have slaves like ancient Athens, which made it easy for public citizens. But we have an affluent society and a lot of spare time.[18]

Mr. Nader went on in the interview to delineate three citizenship obligations: First, on the job, employees have to be willing to blow the whistle on issues of corporate ethics. Second, there is the "part-time citizen—the person who's the community activist on Saturdays and evenings." And third, "there's the full-time citizenship. I really literally want to see 5,000 public interest lawyers in this town [Washington] in six years. It's just got to be that big. At least a one-to-two ratio compared with private interest lawyers. And also all around the country."[19]

Funding for such full-time "public citizen" efforts would come from foundations, government, and individual contributors, he said. "Tremendous amounts will come in in $5 and $10 bills."[20]

As a sort of primer for citizen action, Ralph Nader's Congress Watch published *Who Runs Congress?* in 1972, which reached No. 1 on *The New York Times* "Bestseller List." The book was chiefly written by Congress Watch Director Mark Green, who ran for Congress in 1980 unsuccessfully against Republican incumbent Bill Green in the silk-stocking district of the Upper East Side of Manhattan.

"Nothing compares with the Congress as the initiating hope of reclaiming America. By reclaiming the Congress, America revolutionizes itself," Mr. Nader says in the Introduction, dated July 1979, for the revised, third edition of *Who Runs Congress?*[21]

Congress made many procedural reforms following the 1972 publication of the Congress Watch report, but Mr. Nader and others in the "public interest" movement expressed disappointment that Congress did not go on to pass "responsive legislation" on such issues as energy, taxes, health insurance, consumer protection, inflation, and unemployment.[22]

"For those who have *experienced* the dynamics of organized power groups acting on the Congressional process . . . the failure of procedural improvements to thwart special interest demands or advance public interest values confirms again that the roots of Congressional behavior lie more in the economy than in the polity," Mr. Nader writes in his 1979 Introduction.[23] "Looming over Capitol Hill," he says, "are the omnipresent and relentless demands of corporate power. It is the strongest force working on the Congress."[24]

To counterpoise such corporate lobbying, Mr. Nader says there is a "fundamental necessity of a knowledgeable and involved citizen action process streaming regularly toward Congress from all over the country and from Washington-based [public interest] centers."[25] The American people must, he adds, "care about what they've lost to Congress so that they can take more of it back for the good of themselves, their fellow citizens, and their children."[26]

Congress Watch, which produced the book, leaves little to chance about its effort to solicit support for its efforts in influencing Congress. At the back of the revised edition of *Who Runs Congress?* is a list of "useful materials to assist you [the reader] in monitoring and contributing to Congressional policies on the important issues of the eighties." These "materials" comprise "teacher guides," publications, and newspapers from several of Mr. Nader's organizations.[27]

THE PRESENT

The style and focus of Mr. Nader and some of his network organizations have changed markedly in recent years. In celebration of the 10th anniversary of Public Citizen, Inc., for instance, the group held a "gala" $1,000-a-plate fund-raising dinner in Washington in September 1981. Preparations were made for about 400 guests.[28] The "gala" was accompanied by a two-day conference titled "Taking Charge: The Next 10 Years," at which Mr. Nader expressed hope that the Reagan administration will be his next Corvair. The administration's "disastrous, anti-consumer policies," he said, may galvanize citizens to rebuild the stalled consumer movement.[29]

The conference outlined a shift in Mr. Nader's consumer programs away from federal health and safety regulation and toward greater consumer control of broadcast airwaves, public lands, and pension funds. Mr. Nader also talked of plans to help organize local "consumer utility boards" to monitor utility operations and electricity and gas rate increases.

Two common threads run through Mr. Nader's statements and the activities of his attendant organizations: "corporate accountability" and "citizen power." Corporations should disclose more information about their internal operations and their products to the public, adhere more strictly to the law and governmental regulations, and allow greater public involvement in their decision-making processes. The average citizen should take a greater interest in public affairs in general and in operations of corporations in particular. Moreover, a professional elite of "full-time citizens" is needed to protect the "public interest."

The Capital Legal Foundation's investigation into the Nader network revealed, however, that his groups do not live by the tenets of accountability which Mr. Nader advocates for corporations. Disclosure of information is closely guarded, laws and regulations concerning the operation of these groups have been disregarded, and the general public is infrequently asked to participate in their "public interest" movement. The groups maintain an elitist view of their operations and purposes. The term "public interest," which has never been defined clearly, is often invoked to support causes and activities that are really of a "special interest" nature, such as greater regulation of businesses and the economy by government, and less free enterprise.

Capital Legal Foundation uncovered a Nader network of 19 closely tied corporations and trusts, all of which are tax-exempt and many of which are entitled to receive tax-deductible contributions from individuals, foundations, and companies. The most powerful and important members of this network were directly controlled or completely under the influence of Mr. Nader and no one else. In fact, of the entire 19 groups, only one is a membership organization, and it does not play a large role in the network. The key members of the network operate with immense freedom from public scrutiny and control.

Several of the major organizations in the network, including the most important two—the Center for the Study of Responsive Law (CSRL) and Public Citizen—contrived to disregard the charitable solicitation laws in 25 states. These require registration of groups before they solicit funds in these states. At least one state, New York, had to pursue CSRL and Public Citizen in order to try and force them to obey these laws, which are designed to protect the public from fraud and misrepresentation.

This hypocrisy was also reflected in the secrecy with which the network shrouds all its operations and finances. Few of the organizations publish substantial public reports on their activities or finances; those that are published are too vague and sketchy to provide adequate information on their activities. Furthermore, these organizations refused to respond to repeated requests by telephone and in writing for more information about who controlled them, what their policies were, and how they operated. Such vagueness and refusals to disclose information say much about the attitude of people who argue so stridently for more openness on the part of government and businesses. More specifically, what is the network trying to hide?

It is likely that it is trying to hide the substantial wealth and power that the groups have arrogated to themselves in the last decade or more. Six of the network organizations, including those over which Mr. Nader had the closest control and most direct involvement, had aggregate annual gross receipts of approximately $1.9 million in 1978. This is not a picture of weak, thinly financed, or ineffective organizations. Rather, it is an outline of a large, effective, and well-financed lobbying group which is dug into the nation's capital and well-organized to pursue its ends while simultaneously deflecting public attention from its size and power.

Furthermore, ancillary groups annually raise a substantial amount of money at colleges and universities throughout the country through a "negative check-off" device. At many schools, part of every student's association dues are automatically assigned to a local Public Interest Research Group (PIRG). The students cannot prevent their money from being allocated to a PIRG. The best they can do is to file a claim with the college to obtain a refund. The negative check-off device was conceived by Mr. Nader's Public Interest Research Group and is a principal fund-raising tool of campus-based PIRGs.

This oppressive device, which relies for its success on student apathy or inertia, is currently under attack by some students in the courts. Mr. Nader himself would not approve of businesses, such as record and book clubs, that use it. Yet neither he nor any network group has ever criticized or disavowed its use to fund local PIRGs. There is obviously no reluctance on the Nader network's part to use this unfair method of fund-raising, provided the fruits of its use benefit "public interest" groups and not business.

Capital Legal Foundation was unable to identify the "public" whose interests the network organizations supposedly represent. The groups generally eschew public membership, and hence avoid any risk that outsiders and contributors can direct their operations and determine their policies. Less than one-third of the funds of the network groups, whose finances were examined in detail, comes from the public. The rest comes from several private foundations, the network's assets—which were amassed in large part with money squirreled away from tax-deductible contributions from the general public—and from Mr. Nader's substantial personal earnings.

The tax-exempt status of these groups has facilitated their fund-raising efforts, but in many cases this status has not precluded them from lobbying for political causes in the halls of government or the chambers on Capitol Hill. In the opinion of the Capital Legal Foundation, the network has trod upon thin ice where its tax-exempt status is concerned. It has been cited several times by the Internal Revenue Service for improper churning of its corporate assets. Moreover, it has built an interrelated structure of tax-exempt research and lobbying groups whose propinquity in our opinion may effectively permit financing of some lobbying activities from tax-deductible contributions, even though contributions to lobbying groups are not supposed to be deductible for tax purposes. With consummate cheek, one of the network's major groups maintains a division exclusively concerned with modifying tax laws.

Inconsistency between the network's public positions and its own practices is a common thread in its operations. Thus, while Mr. Nader calls for more disclosure of government activities and is willing to break the economic spine of business with unproductive and useless reporting requirements, he has specifically and vigorously lobbied against increased disclosure and reporting requirements for "public interest" organizations such as his own.

Another shocking example of hypocrisy is the investment policy of some of the network groups. For example, some have campaigned vigorously against corporations in which *other* network groups hold stock and from whose activities they profit. Some of the network groups conducted short sales in stocks—that is, sold stocks they did not own—of companies which they investigated or which were about to be publicly chastised. These network organizations never publicized their investment practices.

Capital Legal Foundation's research unearthed a highly reticulated group of small corporations and trusts, joined together by law or fealty to one person. It is a network of vaguely named organizations, its boards largely composed of the same persons, and its funding furnished from a few rather than many sources. Thus, the criticisms of interlocking directorates, centralization and concentration of power, waste and unrepresentativeness that Mr. Nader uses to castigate other groups and businesses are the very same qualities that characterize the construction and control of his own, less visible empire.

The empire's purposes remain vague, because the groups are reluctant to make known their ambitions and ideology in anything but the broadest outline. In the course of its research, the Capital Legal Foundation did note that the network organizations spend little time on such matters as civil rights or assistance for the poor. Mr. Nader himself, and some of his key associates were educated in Eastern prep schools and the finest of the private Ivy League universities. In these cases, inherited wealth gives them the freedom to upbraid those institutions that often provide the less fortunate with new opportunities for advancement.

What is clear is that Mr. Nader and his network distrust the current political and economic system in the United States, and seek to change it. They do not put much faith in the democratic process that has been America's unique tradition for the past 200 years—that is, the political votes we cast regularly at the ballot box, and the economic votes we make every day with our money at the cash register, at the bank or in the investment markets. Our diverse, de-centralized political, economic, and social system, with its heavy reliance on individual choice, is not considered adequate to achieve the "public interest" or the "common good."

Instead, Mr. Nader and his groups seek a greater politicalization of life in America, where more decisions will be made by a few to affect the many. Government would have an especially large influence on the functioning of the economy and, in turn, on our daily lives. In this regard, a new elite of un-elected, professional "public interest" advocates would acquire a substantial amount of power to make decisions in both the private and public sectors.

In sum, America would become a more centrally governed and less free, individualistic nation. "Public interest" advocates would become new power-brokers, and their ideology would have immense impact on political and economic activities and society as a whole. Ralph Nader seeks nothing less than a transfer of power in America, away from the individual and into the hands of the government and "public interest" groups.

NOTES

1. Nader, Ralph, *Unsafe at Any Speed* (Grossman, New York), 1965.

2. *New York Times,* Nov. 30, 1965, p. 68.

3. *New York Times,* Dec. 1, 1965, p. 37, and April 16, 1966, p. 1.

4. *New York Times,* March 6, 1966, p. 94.

5. Ibid.

6. *New York Times,* March 9, 1966, p. 38.

7. *New York Times,* March 10, 1966, p. 1.

8. Ibid.

9. *New York Times,* March 23, 1966, p. 1.

10. *New York Times,* Nov. 17, 1966, p. 35.

11. *New York Times,* Aug. 14, 1970, p. 1.

12. *New York Times,* Jan. 24, 1971, Sec. 3, pp. 1, 9.

13. Ibid.

14. Ibid.

15. Ibid.

16. Ibid.

17. Ibid.

18. Ibid.

19. Ibid.

20. Ibid.

21. Green, Mark, *Who Runs Congress?* (Bantam Books, New York), rev. 3rd ed., 1979, p. xviii.

22. Ibid., pp. xi-xii.

23. Ibid., p. xi.

24. Ibid., p. xiv.

25. Ibid., p. xv.

26. Ibid., p. xvi.

27. Ibid., pp. xix, 345, & 346.

28. *New York Times*, Sept. 26, 1981, Sec. 1, p. 31.

29. Ibid.

Chapter 2
Constituent
Organizations

Does a "Nader network" in fact exist as has been reported in the press?[1] If so, how many organizations does this "network" include and what are they? What are their policies and programs? What is the nature of their relationship to each other?

These were the first questions the Capital Legal Foundation sought to answer in conducting its study. It soon discovered that no single reference source existed with complete, up-to-date answers. It therefore consulted a variety of sources, including biographical and journalistic accounts, legal documents and organizational literature, and as well conducted a series of interviews. (More information on research techniques and interviews is included in appendices A and B.)

For reasons of clarity and textual organization, this and subsequent chapters will follow a format of first laying out the facts and then drawing conclusions.

FACTS

Nineteen organizations were found to comprise the "Nader network." Ten are primary groups with distinct legal status: Americans Concerned About Corporate Power; Aviation Consumer Action Project; Center for Study of Responsive Law; Corporate Accountability Research Group; Equal Justice Foundation; National Citizens Committee for Broadcasting; Public Citizen, Inc.; Public Interest Research Group; Public Safety Research Institute; and Safety Systems Foundation.

The remaining nine are semi-autonomous subgroups of Public Citizen, Inc., and the Center for the Study of Responsive Law. Although these subgroups have distinct organizational identities, they lack independent legal and tax status.

Public Citizen has six subgroups, which are described as "program areas"[2]: (1) Congress Watch; (2) Critical Mass Energy Project; (3) Health Research Group; (4) Litigation Group; (5) Tax Reform Research Group; (6) and Visitors Center. The subdivisions under the Center for the Study of Responsive Law are: (1) Citizens Utility Board; (2) Freedom of Information Clearinghouse; and (3) Learning Research Project. (Unless otherwise indicated or where obviously inappropriate, the primary organizations and subgroups will be treated as separate entities. In instances where tax or legal status is particularly relevant, the network will be deemed to consist of 10 organizations rather than 19.)

The organizations vary in terms of origin, purpose, structure and degree of affiliation with Mr. Nader. Some engage in lobbying and others are strictly research-oriented. Their concerns range from such general aims as "the common good and general welfare"[3] to more specific issues such as tax reform and environmental regulation.

Despite their diversity, the groups are highly integrated and can be accurately described as a "network" based on the following factors: shared offices and personnel, interlocking directorates, interorganizational income transfers, legal relationships, and a common affiliation with Ralph Nader.

To facilitate analysis of the nature and interrelationships of the network, the constituent groups are broadly classified below in terms of activities, interests, and organizational structure. Individual data on the groups are laid out in detail in Appendix C. It should be emphasized that the appendices are an integral, substantive part of the report; they are separated here in the interests of clarity.

Activities

Network organizations engage principally in four activities: research, information dissemination, litigation, and lobbying.

Research is the primary activity of four network organizations.[4] Twelve groups, including most of the research outfits, engage in substantial information dissemination or "public education."[5] Seven groups regularly publish newsletters, magazines, and reports.[6]

Approximately five organizations are substantially involved in litigation.[7] At least one group, Public Citizen's Litigation Group, considers litigation its chief function.

Five network groups[8] include lobbying among their major activities. These groups lobby primarily with regard to legislation that is germane to their organizational purposes. For example, in 1978 the Aviation Consumer Action Project lobbied for legislation pertaining to economic regulation of airlines,[9] while the Tax Reform Research Group sought to influence "general legislation concerning the IRS and federal fiscal tax policy."[10]

The various subgroups that comprise Public Citizen, Inc., engage in a significant amount of lobbying. They had a total of 13 registered lobbyists as of the first quarter of 1980.[11] Eight worked for Congress Watch, two at Health Research, and one each at Critical Mass Energy Project, Tax Reform Research Group, and Litigation Group.

In addition to congressional lobbying, five network groups act as advocates before federal regulatory agencies. These are Aviation Consumer Action Project, National Citizens Committee for Broadcasting, Critical Mass Energy Project, Health Research Group, and the Tax Reform Research Group.

Interests

The substantive goals of the network organizations include government regulation of industry, open government and greater citizens' participation, occupational health and safety, environmental protection, legal services for the poor, and greater aid for the public interest movement as a whole.

Government regulation of corporations is a primary concern of eight network organizations.[12] Three groups—Americans Concerned About Corporate Power, the Corporate Accountability Research Group, and the Public Interest Research Group—were specifically organized to advocate federal regulation of the private sector. Nader states that corporations should be regulated because of their "high concentration of power."[13]

So-called "open government" and greater citizen access to the governmental decision-making processes are advocated by six of the network organizations.[14] Congress Watch, for example, lobbied in Congress in favor of strengthening the Freedom of Information Act, which permits citizen access to a vast array of government documents and files that otherwise would have been kept confidential.[15] The Center for Study of Responsive Law established the Freedom of Information Clearinghouse for the express purpose of helping citizens obtain information from the government under the act.[16]

Improved occupational safety, through increased federal regulation, is a goal of four network organizations.[17] Two network units—Critical Mass Energy Project and Congress Watch—advocate environmental protection. Mr. Nader says that corporations are to blame for many of our environmental problems. "Corporations," he says, "tell us what kind of air, water, and soil we'll have."[18]

Congress Watch and Critical Mass Energy Project specifically oppose nuclear energy development.[19] It's a view shared by Mr. Nader: "Shouldn't you destroy property before it destroys you? . . . If they don't close these reactors down, we'll have civil war within five years."[20]

The Equal Justice Foundation promotes the interests of the economically disadvantaged. In particular, the groups seek to provide legal services to the poor.

Finally, five network organizations[21] assist *other* public interest groups. Aid often takes the form of grants. The awarding of grants constitutes the major activity of groups such as the Public Safety Research Institute and the Safety Systems Foundation; Public Citizen and the Center for the Study of Responsive Law have also made grants to numerous public interest organizations. The Nader groups also provide advice, information, and help to mobilize resources to other public interest organizations.

Organization Structure

The network groups' organizational structure, meaning their form of legal organization and tax status, also merits discussion. It provides an insight into the advantages and disadvantages of holding tax-exempt status.

At least eight[22] of the network organizations qualify for some degree of tax exemption under the Internal Revenue Code of 1954.[23] Seven of the tax-exempt groups (all except Public Citizen) qualify as tax-exempt under Section 501 (c) (3) of the Internal Revenue Code of 1954. In pertinent part, Section 501 (c) (3) grants exemption to:

> Corporations, and any community chest, fund or foundation, organized and operated exclusively for religious, charitable, scientific testing for public safety, literary, or educational purposes, or to foster national or international amateur sports competition (but only if no part of its activities involve the provision of athletic facilities or equipment), or for the prevention of cruelty to children or animals . . . .

An important attribute of Section 501 (c) (3) status is that contributions to qualifying groups are deductible by the donor and non-taxable to the donee.[24]

While these dual benefits certainly make fund raising easier for such organizations, 501 (c) (3) status is not without disadvantages. It also provides that "no substantial part of the activities"[25] of organizations exempt under provisions may constitute "carrying on propaganda, or otherwise attempting, to influence legislation." Thus, organizations qualifying under Section 501 (c) (3) are not allowed to "participate in, or intervene in (including the publishing or distributing of statements), any political campaign on behalf of any candidate for public office." While 501 (c) (3) organizations enjoy important fund-raising advantages, their lobbying and electoral activities are severely circumscribed.

One network group, Public Citizen, qualifies as tax-exempt under Section 501 (c) (4) of the I.R.S. Code. In pertinent part, Section 501 (c) (4) of the Code exempts:

> civic leagues or organizations not organized for profit but operated exclusively for the promotion of social welfare. . . .

Section 501 (c) (4) groups are exempt from federal income taxation like 501 (c) (3) groups. However, contributions to 501 (c) (4) organizations are not deductible by the donor for federal tax purposes. Although this limitation places such organizations at a disadvantage insofar as fund raising is concerned, they are permitted—unlike Section 501 (c) (3) groups—to engage in lobbying activities.[26]

At least six network groups are corporations.[27] Five were incorporated under the laws of the District of Columbia.[28] Public Safety Research Institute was organized in Delaware.

Two network groups are trusts: the Center for the Study of Responsive Law, which was established in the District of Columbia, and the Safety Systems Foundation, which was created in New York.

CONCLUSIONS

It is our opinion that the formal distinctions between lobbying and non-lobbying groups [503 (c) (3) vs. 503 (c) (4)] are more apparent than real. The "research" conducted by network groups is not undertaken for academic or descriptive purposes. In our view, the research is used to promote a particular policy or legislative outcome, albeit by other network groups which are formally authorized to engage in lobbying. Despite formal distinctions, there is a symbiotic relationship between the "research" and "lobbying" groups—that is, one hand washes the other.

A plausible explanation for the formal separation of these groups is that some groups do not wish to disclose the true extent of their lobbying because of tax considerations and public image. Lobbying is the prime means of promoting special interests and generally has a negative connotation. Since lobbying by corporate interests is often criticized, the network is loath to admit using these same techniques.

As previously noted, several network groups and Mr. Nader advocate regulation of corporations. In our estimation, Mr. Nader and these groups seem more concerned with the quantity of corporate regulation than the quality, and fail to consider the cost and / or necessity of further regulation. It appears that regulation of corporate activity is an ultimate network goal rather than a means of furthering legitimate societal interests. The views of the groups that advocate corporate regulation comport well with Mr. Nader's personal abhorrence of corporations, which, according to Mr. Nader, should be regulated because of their "high concentrations of power."[29]

To a large extent, this preoccupation with corporate regulation demonstrates an indifference to the legitimate requirements of economic development and reflects a distinctive world view. That is, the conceptual world of the groups is discernibly polarized when viewed as a contest between corporations, which should be regulated, and the self-proclaimed defenders of "the public interest," who should be promoted.

Several groups, including CSRL and several sub-groups of Public Citizen, purport to favor governmental and business accountability, open government, and the free flow of information. CSRL and Public Citizen do not always acknowledge reciprocal duties of openness, disclosure, and accountability. Rather, these groups have a one-sided view of public disclosure and open government, as their refusal to submit to public scrutiny or otherwise make pertinent facts concerning their operations available to the public demonstrates.

Mr. Nader castigates corporations and attributes many environmental problems to them. And, of course, there is a panacea for all these ills: more corporate regulation. Apparently there is no such thing as bad regulation or a non-regulatory solution.

No one seriously disputes the fact that safety and environmental issues are entitled to thoughtful consideration. However the solution will not always be found in the Code of Federal Regulations. Rather, a solution to the problem depends on an analytical framework that considers cost, benefits, and tradeoffs.

Mr. Nader seems unwilling to undertake the requisite balancing analysis as his stance on nuclear power demonstrates, that is, solve the nuclear problem by closing down reactors. Complex environmental problems cannot be analyzed and solved with a reductionist approach which holds that corporations are responsible; regulate corporations and the problems will disappear. This reductionist approach is patently irresponsible and vacuous.

NOTES

1. See, for example, Gross, "The Nader Network," 13 *Business and Society Rev.* 5-15 (1975); "Mr. Nader's Conglomerate," *Wall Street Journal,* April 17, 1980, at 26; Clark, "After a Decade of Doing Battle, Public Interest Groups Show Their Age," *National Journal,* June 12, 1980, at 1136-41; Jacquency, "The Washington Pressures / Nader network switches focus to legal action, congressional lobbying," *National Journal,* June 9, 1973.

2. Telephone conversation with Emma Smith, accountant for Public Citizen and the Center for Study of Responsive Law (June 2, 1980).

3. Public Citizen, Inc., Articles of Incorporation.

4. Center for Study of Responsive Law, Congress Watch, Corporate Accountability Research Group, Tax Reform Research Group.

5. Americans Concerned About Corporate Power, Center for Study of Responsive Law, Congress Watch, Accountability Research Group, Critical Mass Energy Project, Equal Justice Foundation, Health Research Group, National Citizen's Committee for Broadcasting, Learning Research Project, Public Citizen Visitors Center, Public Interest Research Group, Tax Reform Research Group.

6. Center for Study of Responsive Law, Congress Watch, Corporate Accountability Research Group, Critical Mass Energy Project, National Citizens Visitors Center, Public Interest Research Group, Tax Reform Research Group.

7. Aviation Consumers Action Project, Center for Study of Responsive Law, Health Research Group, Public Citizen Litigation Group, Tax Reform Research Group.

8. Congress Watch, Critical Mass Energy Project, Health Research Group, Public Citizen Litigation Group, Tax Reform Research Group. (Aviation Consumer Project has engaged in lobbying in the past.)

9. Lobbyist Registration Forms filed with the Clerk of the House of

Representatives by Mimi Cutler, Cornish Hitchcock and ACAP in 1978 and 1979.

10. Lobbyist Registration Forms filed with the Clerk of the House of Representatives by TRRG in 1978 and 1979.

11. Registered with the Secretary of the Senate and the Clerk of the House of Representatives of the United States Congress.

12. Americans Concerned about Corporate Power, Aviation Consumer Action Project, Citizen Utility Board, Corporate Accountability Research Group, Critical Mass Energy Project, National Citizens Committee for Broadcasting, Public Interest Research Group, Tax Reform Research Group.

13. Speech by Ralph Nader to Congressional Interns (June 12, 1980).

14. Aviation Consumer Action Project, Congress Watch, Center for Study of Responsive Law, Equal Justice Foundation, Public Citizen Litigation Group, Public Citizen Visitors Center.

15. Public Citizen's 1979 Annual Report.

16. Statement mailed upon request to Capital Legal Foundation by Lorraine Thal of the Clearinghouse, received 7/11/80.

17. Aviation Consumer Action Project, Congress Watch, Health Research Group, Public Citizen Litigation Group.

18. Speech by Nader to Congressional Interns (June 12, 1980).

19. Richard Pollock, "Working for a Safe Energy Future," *The Public Citizen*, Issue Eleven, Winter 1980, p. 2; Lobbying Registration Forms filed with the Clerk of the House of Representatives by Congress Watch in 1979.

20. Anna Mayo, "Geiger Counter," *The Village Voice*, April 4, 1977, at 33.

21. Center for Study of Responsive Law, Citizens Utility Board, Public Citizen, Public Safety Research Institute, Safety Systems Foundations.

22. Americans Concerned About Corporate Power, Aviation Consumer Action Project, Center for Study of Responsive Law,

Equal Justice Foundation, National Citizens Committee for Broadcasting, Public Citizen, Public Safety Research Institute, Safety Systems Foundation.

23. The ten subgroups operated by Public Citizen and the Center for Study of Responsive Law, are not considered separate units within the context of this statement.

24. Under IRS Sections 170 (c) (2), 2055 (a) (2), and 2522 (b) (2).

25. See Hopkins B., *The Law of Tax-Exempt Organizations* (3rd ed. 1979), Ch. 13 (Tax Reform Act of 1976 sought to define vague phrase "no substantial part" by limiting financial expenditures organizations could make for legislative activities).

26. However, like 501 (c) (3) groups, 501 (c) (4) organizations are prohibited from engaging in campaign activities.

27. Americans Concerned About Corporate Power, Aviation Consumer Action Project, Equal Justice Foundation, National Citizens Committee for Broadcasting, Public Citizen, Public Safety Research Institute.

28. Americans Concerned About Corporate Power, Aviation Consumer Action Project, Equal Justice Foundation, National Citizens Committee for Broadcasting, Public Citizen.

29. Speech by Ralph Nader to Congressional Interns (June 12, 1980).

Chapter 3
Links Between Nader and Network Groups

In all the time Ralph Nader has been in the public eye, his precise affiliation with many of the public interest groups that are commonly associated with his name has never been made clear. How much direct control or involvement in these groups does he really have?

One of the principal objectives of the Capital Legal Foundation study was to determine the scope and breadth of the Nader network. To this end, we tried to ascertain the nature of the links between the constituent groups and the nature of their links to Mr. Nader.

In response to the foundation's inquiries, spokespersons for Mr. Nader claimed that he is only affiliated with two groups—Public Citizen, Inc. (inclusive of its six subgroups), and the Center for the Study of Responsive Law (inclusive of its three subgroups).[1] These spokespersons later acknowledged that Mr. Nader is also affiliated with two other groups—the Public Interest Research Group and the Corporate Accountability Research Group. Because these initial responses were less than forthcoming, Capital decided to conduct independent research.

FACTS

Ralph Nader held as of October 1, 1980, a legal or managerial position, such as trustee, director, or executive officer, or contributed funds to ten groups and nine subgroups that make up the Nader network.

The organizations directly affiliated with Mr. Nader are:

Public Citizen, Inc. Mr. Nader had been President and Treasurer of Public Citizen since its inception in 1971[2] and also served as one of its three directors.[3] The executive directors of Public Citizen's six subgroups report directly to Mr. Nader.[4] Mike Horrocks, Director of Public Citizen's Visitors Center, stated that Mr. Nader controls Public Citizen.[5] However, shortly before Capital completed the first draft of its report on October 28, 1980, Mr. Nader resigned from his position as president of Public Citizen.

Public Citizen serves as the umbrella group for Mr. Nader's lobbying efforts. It funds and operates six subgroups, each of which conducts activities of its own in accordance with Public Citizen's general purpose. Public Citizen also funds other like-minded organizations.

The Center for Study of Responsive Law. Mr. Nader was Managing Trustee[6] of the Center for Study of Responsive Law and has been a Trustee of the organization since its formation as a trust in 1968.[7]

Two other trustees are relatives of Mr. Nader— Mrs. Laura Nader Milleron of Berkeley, California, is his sister, and Mr. Edward Shaker of Toronto, Canada, is his cousin.[8] Nader spokespersons concede that Nader controls the organization.[9]

The Center operates primarily as a research and educational organization.[10] In the past it has been a source of Nader study group reports. The Center has also provided funding to other organizations in the Nader network.[11]

Public Interest Research Group and Corporate Accountability Research Group. Mr. Nader wholly funds the Public Interest Research Group and the Corporate Accountability Research Group with his own income.[12] Although Mr. Nader does not hold a titled position with these organizations, he "runs [them] because he pays the salaries."[13]

The major activity of PIRG and CARG is presently the publication of the *Multinational Monitor* magazine, which reports on the activities of multinational corporations.[14] The magazine's listed phone number is that of the Nader-controlled Center for Study of Responsive Law.

Public Safety Research Institute. The Public Safety Research Institute is a tax-exempt private foundation[15] which was incorporated under the laws of Delaware in 1968. Mr. Nader serves as president, treasurer and as one of three members on the board of directors.[16] The two remaining board members are cousins of Mr. Nader—Edmund and Diana Shaker of Toronto, Canada.[17] Mr. Shaker also serves as a trustee of the Center for Study of Responsive Law.[18]

A major activity of this organization is making grants to other organizations, several of which are controlled by Mr. Nader.

Safety Systems Foundation. Safety Systems Foundation was formed as a trust in 1966 in New York.[19] Mr. Nader's sister, Laura Nader Milleron, has been the sole trustee of the foundation since its formation.[20] Theodore Jacobs is listed as "Donor" in the Trust Agreement.[21] Mr. Jacobs was also the "Donor" listed in CSRL's Trust Agreement.[22]

According to Forms 990 filed by Safety Systems with the Internal Revenue Service, Mr. Nader has been the sole contributor to the Foundation since its inception.[23] He has given more than $212,000 to Safety Systems during the past 12 years.[24] The trust was apparently formed with such contributions in mind; Safety Systems' Form 1023 (Exemption Application), filed with the IRS on January 26, 1967, stated: "It is anticipated that in excess of ten (10%) percent of the assets of the trust will be donated by members of the family of trustee Laura Milleron." Supplementary information provided by Safety Systems to the IRS on April 27, 1967, further states that:

> Ralph Nader . . . has indicated his willingness to act in an advisory capacity in the general work of the Foundation and in the selection of research projects to be carried on by the Foundation.

The only apparent activities of Safety Systems are the making of grants to other public-interest organizations, some of which are directly controlled by Mr. Nader, and engaging in speculative stock transactions.

National Citizens Committee for Broadcasting. Mr. Nader serves as Chairman of the Board of Directors of the National Citizens Committee for Broadcasting.[25] An NCCB spokesman confirmed that Mr. Nader has served as Chairman of their Board of Directors since October 1978, adding that NCCB operates with "relative autonomy" from other Nader groups.[26]

NCCB is a membership organization primarily concerned with gaining access to regulatory processes affecting the broadcast media.[27]

The Aviation Consumer Action Project. Nader spokespersons told us that the Aviation Consumer Action Project is no longer affiliated with Mr. Nader or Public Citizen, although they acknowledged that Public Citizen has made grants to ACAP in the past.[28]

An ACAP official informed us, however, that Mr. Nader currently serves as Chairman of ACAP's Advisory Board, upon which it places "strong reliance for advice."[29] Mr. Nader has been "closely involved" with ACAP since its inception, the official added. In addition, a staff attorney with Public Citizen's Litigation Group, Mr. John Cary Sims, served as a member of the board of directors and D.C.-registered agent of the Aviation Consumer Action group.

Examination of the Forms 990 filed by ACAP with the IRS shows that the Nader-controlled Public Citizen, Inc., has been ACAP's major contributor in the past. Between 1974 and 1978, for example, Public Citizen gave $146,735 to ACAP,[30] thus providing almost 80 percent of the $188,162 in total contributions received by ACAP during that period.[31] Also, in 1979 Public Citizen contributed an additional $27,523 to ACAP, which made ACAP the sole recipient of Public Citizen's grants for that year.[32] Safety Systems Foundation—to which Mr. Nader is the sole contributor—made an $8,000 grant to ACAP in 1979.[33]

Thus Mr. Nader has been connected with ACAP in an indirect manner through his control of Public Citizen, which funnels funds to ACAP, as well as in a direct advisory capacity.

The interests and activities of ACAP revolve

around advocacy of passenger interests before federal regulatory agencies and the courts. ACAP has also lobbied in Congress on legislation concerning airline regulation.[34]

Americans Concerned about Corporate Power. Mr. Nader is also directly connected with Americans Concerned about Corporate Power. He is listed as an "Initiating Sponsor" and member of the Advisory Board of the "Big Business Day Committee," which is another name for the Americans Concerned About Corporate Power[35] that reflects its role in sponsoring the anticorporation "Big Business Day" on April 17, 1980.

In addition, Mr. Mark Green, then Director of Public Citizen's Congress Watch, served as Chairman of the Board of Directors of Americans Concerned About Corporate Power[36] from its inception until spring 1980, when he resigned to make an unsuccessful bid for Congress.

Michael Jacobson, Ph.D., a former employee of the Center for Study of Responsive Law, has been a Director and D.C.-registered agent of Americans Concerned about Corporate Power since its inception.[37] He has also served as Secretary-Treasurer of the group.[38]

Public Citizen, Inc., co-authored with Americans Concerned About Corporate Power a document entitled "The Case for the Corporate Democracy Act," which was released at a press conference on December 12, 1979.

ACACP seeks to inform the public of alleged corporate abuses of power and the purported insensitivity of corporations to the needs of the community.[39]

Equal Justice Foundation. There remains an additional organization to which Mr. Nader is now directly connected—The Equal Justice Foundation. As Mr. Nader recently wrote, "In 1978, together with a number of public interest lawyers, I joined with students from a growing number of law schools to establish the Equal Justice Foundation."[40] A spokesperson for the Foundation also noted that Nader was involved in its formation, characterizing the Foundation as a "Nader spinoff."[41] She noted that Nader currently provides "most" of the Foundation's funds by donating the honoraria he receives from speeches at law schools.[42] The Equal Justice Foundation maintains contact with Mr. Nader which is "regular but not systematic," the spokesperson added.[43]

The organization's activities and concerns are directed toward increasing citizen access to, and representation in, the courts, legislative bodies, and administrative agencies.[44]

CONCLUSIONS

In our opinion, the evidence presented in this chapter and the preceding chapter, "Constituent Organizations," conclusively demonstrates that a Nader network of organizations does exist. The network, which consists of ten primary organizations and nine subgroups, is characterized by interlocking directorates, interorganizational income transfers, shared personnel and facilities, and shared ideology. Although the network consists of many seemingly diverse groups, they all exhibit a common denominator—namely, a discernible and direct affiliation with Mr. Nader.

The numerical strength of the network tends to give the impression of a broad base of popular support. However, the National Citizens Committee for Broadcasting is the only membership organization in the network. As far as Capital's research could determine, only one network group—Public Citizen, Inc.—enjoys a measurable amount of direct public support. The other network groups are primarily supported by private foundation funding, Mr. Nader's personal income, income transfers among various network organizations, and income from government bonds and investments.

These network organizations, in our view, are merely pawns in a sophisticated version of the old "shell game"—"Now you see it. Now you don't." When it is desirable to present a façade of broad-based public support, the breadth and scope of the network is exaggerated. On other occasions, when it is advantageous to depict the network as a bedraggled army of public-minded servants fighting against insurmountable odds, the scope is de-emphasized. The network's scope is similarly denigrated when it is advantageous to downplay its economic resources. (But more on finances will come in a subsequent chapter).

In sum, investigation of the constituent organizations of the Nader network and their direct links with Ralph Nader belies the impression they seek to foster of a heterogeneous grouping interested only in the "public interest" or "common good." A more accurate impression is one of a small insular community, advocating a common ideological cause, and joined by a common bond in the person of Ralph Nader.

NOTES

1. Mike Horrocks, Director of Public Citizen's Visitor Center—interview, 6/5/80. Emmy Smith, accountant for Public Citizen and the Center for Study of Responsive Law—phone conversation, 6/1/80.

2. Mr. Nader resigned from his position as President of Public Citizen. See "Ralph Nader Resigns From Consumer Post," *Washington Post*, 10/28/80.

3. Public Citizen, Inc., Articles of Incorporation.

4. Statement by Mike Horrocks, Director of Public Citizen's Visitors Center—interview, 6/5/80.

5. Statement by Mike Horrocks, Director of Public Citizen's Visitors Center—interview, 6/5/80.

6. Form 990 filed with the IRS in May 1978.

7. CSRL's Trust Agreement.

8. Barbara O'Reilly, "Nader Series," written for Gannett News Service, 3/29/79.

9. Mike Horrocks, Director of Public Citizen's Visitor Center—interview, 6/5/80. Emmy Smith, accountant for Public Citizen and the Center for Study of Responsive Law—phone conversation, 6/2/80.

10. CSRL's Trust Agreement. See also Form 1023 Exemption Application filed with the IRS.

11. See generally CSRL's Form 990s filed with the IRS for 1970-78.

12. Mike Horrocks, Director of Public Citizen's Visitor Center—interview, 6/5/80. Emmy Smith, accountant for Public Citizen and the Center for Study of Responsive Law—phone conversation, 6/2/80.

13. Marilyn Osterman, PIRG/CARG Office Manager—phone conversation, 7/8/80.

14. Ibid.

15. The Internal Revenue Service's "Cumulative List" of Organizations described in Section 170 (c) of the Internal Revenue Code of 1954 (i.e., tax-exempt organizations), revised to 1/31/80.

16. Form 990-AR, 1979 Annual Report of Private Foundation filed with the IRS pursuant to Section 6056 of the Internal Revenue Code.

17. Ibid.

18. Form 990 filed by CSRL with the IRS in 1979.

19. Safety System's Trust Agreement was made on November 7, 1966.

20. Laura Milleron was listed as Trustee in the Trust Agreement of 1966 and has been listed as trustee in every IRS return up until the end of 1979.

21. Safety System's Trust Agreement.

22. CSRL's Trust Agreement.

23. Forms 990 filed with the IRS 1967-79.

24. The precise amount that Nader contributed in 1971 was omitted from Safety System's Form 990 filed with the IRS for that year. However, Nader is listed as a substantial contributor for that year. SSF's contributions totaled $15,000 in 1971.

25. NCCB newsletter *Access*, No. 97, May 19, 1980, p. 4. Available at Public Citizen's Visitor Center as of 5/23/80; see also form 990 filed with IRS in November 1979.

26. Statement by Joe Waz, Deputy Director of NCCB, phone conversation, 6/30/80.

27. Form 1023 Application for Exemption filed with the IRS in 1973.

28. Mike Horrocks, Director of Public Citizen's Visitor Center — interview, 6/5/80. Emmy Smith, accountant for Public Citizen and the Center for Study of Responsive Law—phone conversation, 6/3/80.

29. Statement by Kathy Waldbauer, Administrative Assistant with ACAP—phone conversation, 6/26/80.

30. Form 990s filed with the IRS by Public Citizen for 1974-78.

31. Form 990s filed with the IRS by ACAP for 1974-78.

32. Annual Report for 1979 filed with the State of New York.

33. Form 990-AR filed with the IRS for 1979 by Safety Systems Foundation.

34. Lobbying registration forms filed with Clerk of the House of Representatives in 1978.

35. Statement by Charles Garlow, co-director of ACACP—phone conversation, 7/7/80.

36. Ibid.

37. Documents filed with D.C. Corporate Records Office.

38. Ibid.

39. Statement by Charles Garlow, co-director of ACAP—phone conversation, 7/7/80.

40. "Nader," Virginia Law Weekly, *Dicta,* Vol. 32, No. 24 (1980), p. 1.

41. Jennifer McKenna, Office Manager and Researcher at E.J.F.—phone conversation, 6/26/80.

42. Ibid.

43. Ibid.

44. Equal Justice Foundation Brochure distributed at Public Citizen Visitors Center. Obtained 6/5/80.

Chapter 4
Nader and Other Public Interest Groups

During the 1960s and 1970s, the publicity about Ralph Nader's activities helped spawn a popular concern about "consumer" and "public interest" issues in the United States. Although this concern generally had an amorphous quality, there were numerous attempts by various organizers to harness and institutionalize this popular interest. Not all of these efforts were successful. But many gained at least a toe hold in the developing structure of "public interest" organizations, and some continue to attract supporters and funds and have an influence on public opinion and governmental decision-making.

There has only been a nebulous understanding of the relationship of these apparently independent groups with Mr. Nader and his network organizations. In the course of the Capital Legal Foundation's study, however, it found nearly 50 groups that have or had discernible ties to Mr. Nader or his network. Rather than include these groups in the network per se, it was decided to discuss them separately, since their relationship was not considered substantial enough to qualify them for inclusion. But the ties were sufficiently close to warrant a review. For instance, many of the groups were established by Mr. Nader or received funding from network organizations. Others have the same directors as network groups or may be accurately described as "spin-offs" of the network.

FACTS

The nearly 50 groups that have ties to Mr. Nader or his network are:

Consumers Opposed to Inflation in the Necessities. Public Citizen, Inc. is a member of the COIN coalition, which was formed in 1978.[1] The COIN coalition was organized by Public Citizen and the Exploratory Project for Economic Alternatives.[2] The coalition also includes the Consumer Federation of America,[3] the National Gray Panthers, and a number of Public Interest Research Group branches.[4]

As its name implies, the coalition was organized in response to the effect of inflation in the necessities—health care, food, housing and energy. The organization operates on the premise that inflation is caused by industry.

Disability Rights Center. The center was funded by the Nader-controlled Public Safety Research Institute from 1977 to 1979. Safety Systems Foundation, to which Mr. Nader is the sole contributor, also made grants to the center from 1976 to 1979. One of the center's directors, Ralf Hotchkiss, is also the director of the Center for Concerned Engineering, a spin-off of the Center for Auto Safety, which is also associated with Mr. Nader.[5]

The Disability Rights Center is primarily engaged in monitoring the enforcement of civil rights legislation regarding the disabled. It advocates accessible mass transportation for the disabled and the elimination of employment discrimination. It also disseminates information about issues affecting the disabled.

Pension Rights Center. Like the Disability Rights Center, the Pension Rights Center has received funding from the Public Safety Research Institute (PSRI) and Safety Systems Foundation. PSRI made grants to the Center from 1976 to 1979. Safety Systems made a $2,000 grant to the Pension Rights Center in 1979. Public Citizen promoted the Pension Rights Center in its 1979 Annual Report.

The Center works at reforming the nation's retirement income programs and occasionally publishes a small brochure, entitled *Pension Facts.*

Commission for the Advancement of Public Interest Organizations (CAPIO). Mr. Nader's sister Claire is one of three commissioners of CAPIO. CAPIO seeks to support the development and expansion of other public interest organizations. CAPIO avoids concentrating on particular issues, and primarily acts as an information clearing house.

Monsour Medical Foundation. Mr. Nader's brother, Shafeek, has served as the District of Columbia registered agent for Monsour Medical Foundation since May 17, 1974, when it was granted a "Certificate of Authority to Conduct Affairs in the District of Columbia."

William J. Monsour, M.D., an incorporator and current director of the Foundation, also serves as one of CAPIO's three commissioners.

Monsour Medical Foundation funds CAPIO as well. In fiscal year 1975–76, the Monsour Foundation spent $95,973 "in support of Commission for Advancement of Public Interest Organizations."[6] According to a GannettNews Service article, Monsour Medical Foundation made a $5,000 grant to Nader's Center for Study of Responsive Law.[7]

Rosewater Foundation. Robert C. Townsend established the Rosewater Foundation, then known as the Robert C. Townsend Foundation, in 1964. According to Townsend, he transferred the Rosewater Foundation in 1972 to the Public Safety Research Institute, "or to whomever Nader told us to give it to."[8] Control was in fact passed to Mark Green and Peter Petkas, long-time Nader associates who are listed as trustees on Rosewater's 1972 tax return. In 1973, Harvey Jester, bookkeeper for several network groups, replaced Petkas as trustee.

Prior to the transfer, the Rosewater Foundation had been a prime benefactor of Public Safety Research Institute, having awarded it $200,000 in grants. Prior to 1972, the Foundation also made grants to organizations unaffiliated with Ralph Nader. Since the transfer in 1972, however, Rosewater's grants have gone almost exclusively to Nader organizations. For instance, in 1973, the Center for the Study of Responsive Law received a $20,927 grant from Rosewater.[9] In 1974, CSRL reciprocated by making a $14,685 grant to Rosewater.[10] In 1975, CSRL made a $5,000 grant,[11] thus virtually "washing out" the original $20,000 grant. This transaction is unusual insofar as CSRL does not normally make grants to other network groups. Rosewater also gave money to the Anthropology Resource Center of which Nader's sister, Laura Nader Milleron, is a director.[12]

Most of Rosewater's funding after 1972 has come from Stewart Mott, heir to a General Motors fortune. Since 1973 Rosewater has received about $191,327 in contributions. Mr. Mott's $101,200 donation in 1973 constituted Rosewater's total receipts for that year.[13] In

1974, Mr. Mott contributed another $20,000.[14] Rosewater has also received $35,000 in contributions from the Stern Fund. Rosewater's net worth at the end of 1978 was $30,817.

Center for Science in the Public Interest. The Center was incorporated by three former employees of the Center for Study of Responsive Law: Albert J. Fritsch, Ph.D., Michael Jacobson, Ph.D., and James B. Sullivan. CSPI's initial directors also included a fourth ex-employee of the Center for Study of Responsive Law, Kenneth Lasson.[15] Jacobson, Sullivan and Lasson still serve as directors of CSPI. CSPI received a grant from the Center for Study of Responsive Law in 1974.

Although there are no longer any apparent financial connections between CSPI and organizations directly controlled by Mr. Nader, CSPI literature is distributed at Public Citizen's Visitors Center.[16]

CPSI monitors federal agencies that oversee food safety, trade, and nutrition. The organization also publishes a monthly magazine, *Nutrition Action.*

Center for Auto Safety, Inc. The Center for Auto Safety was "started by Mr. Nader,"[17] and originally was a project to monitor the National Highway Traffic Safety Administration.[18] In 1969, Nader hired Lowell Dodge to oversee this project, and he later became an initial director and District of Columbia registered agent for the Center for Auto Safety when it was incorporated the following year.

In 1971, Mr. Nader, Mr. Dodge, and Ralf Hotchkiss co-authored *The Lemon Book: What To Do With Your Bad Car.*[19] Mr. Hotchkiss is Director of the Center for Concerned Engineering, a spin-off from the Center for Auto Safety.[20]

The Center for Auto Safety received grants from

Safety Systems Foundation in 1971 and from the Center for Study of Responsive Law in 1972. It also received substantial funding from the Consumers Union, on whose board of directors Mr. Nader once served.

A close Nader associate, Reuben B. Robertson III,[21] served on the Center for Auto Safety's Board of Directors during 1977 and 1978. The Center's current President, Clarence M. Ditlow III, is a personal friend of Mr. Nader and a former employee of Public Citizen.[22] He maintains "fairly frequent contact" with Mr. Nader.[23]

The Center's activities revolve around its efforts to influence motor vehicle safety standards.

Transportation Consumer Action Project. TCAP has the same officers as the Aviation Consumer Action Project, which is part of the Nader network. In addition, John Cary Sims, a staff attorney with Public Citizen's Litigation Group, serves as TCAP's registered agent in the District of Columbia and was one of its incorporators.

TCAP advocates development of intercity transportation systems and conducts research on this and related issues.

Fund for Constitutional Government. The Fund was financed by the Center for Study of Responsive Law in 1975 and by the Rosewater Foundation in 1976. Stewart Mott, a major contributor to Rosewater, is a member of the Fund's Board of Directors. Theodore Jacobs, a close Nader associate and Executive Director of the Center for Study of Responsive Law until 1975, has also been a project director and vice-president of the Fund. Margaret Gates, director and treasurer of the Center for Women Policy Studies—started with "seed money" from Public Citizen—was also a director of the Fund for Constitutional Government until May, 1980. Edward Greensfelder is an attorney with the Fund and one of its former incorporators, initial directors, registered agents, and secretaries. He has also served as an incorporator, director, and registered agent of the Public Citizen Action Fund.

The Fund for Constitutional Government's current president, assistant secretary, and assistant treasurer is Anne Zill, who was previously an employee of the Nader-funded Congress Project.

The Fund engages in litigation against corporations and the government and has sponsored a variety of programs advocating "honest and open government."

National Resource Center for Consumers of Legal Services. Alan B. Morrison, executive director of Public Citizen's Litigation Group, serves as vice-president of the National Resource Center for Consumers of Legal Services. Sandra DeMent Sterling, a former employee of Public Citizen's Citizen Action Group,[24] served as the Resource Center's Executive Director until October 1967. She was succeeded by acting director, Joanne Pozzo. Jules Bernstein, a director of Americans Concerned about Corporate Power is treasurer of the NRCCLS. In addition, Rhoda Karpatkin, executive director of Consumers Union and a former director of the Center for Auto Safety, serves as a director of the NRCCLS. Another director, James D. Lorenz, is also a director of the Equal Justice Foundation and President of the Council for Public Interest Law.

When NRCCLS operated under its former name, the "National Consumer Resource Center," its directors included Roy Alper, who has also served as a director of the Consumer Federation of America and the California Citizen Action Group.

The National Resource Center for Consumers of Legal Services received a grant from Public Citizen in 1976.

The NRCCLS was formed with the objective of ameliorating the inadequate provision of legal services to the economically disadvantaged.

New Jersey PIRG. A staff attorney with Public Citizen's Litigation Group, John Cary Sims, is currently participating in a pending case on behalf of the Rutgers branch of PIRG. The case, *Galda, et al.* v. *Bloustein, et al.*, was brought by three Rutgers students who are challenging the constitutionality of PIRG's "negative checkoff" funding system.[25] The case is now pending before the U.S. District Court for the District of New Jersey.

The activities of the NJPIRG include lobbying, research, and the dissemination of information on issues such as nuclear power, water quality, women's rights, and truth in testing.

The Council for Public Interest Law. James D. Lorenz, president of the Council for Public Interest Law, is also a director of the Equal Justice Foundation. Mr. Lorenz also serves as a director of the National Resource Center for Consumers of Legal Services as well. Stephanie Savage, the Council's registered agent in the District of Columbia, is also a director and the D.C. registered agent of the Equal Justice Foundation. Charles Halpern, a director of the Council, also serves as a director of the National Resource Center for Consumers of Legal Services.

The Council's activities primarily focus on public interest law funding. Specifically, the Council has filed briefs in actions involving attorneys fees awards to public interest attorneys. The Council has supported the establishment of a more extensive intervenor funding program in government agencies.

New York PIRG. NYPIRG was founded with the assistance of Public Citizen's Citizen Action Group. Its current director, Donald Ross, is the former director of Citizen Action Group. Mr. Ross co-authored with Mr. Nader a PIRG organizing manual, *Action for a Change.* [26] Kerry Barnett, formerly front office manager of the Center for Study of Responsive Law, left the Center in July 1980 to join the Binghamton branch of NYPIRG.

NYPIRG lobbies and conducts research on energy, tax, health, and environmental issues. The organization engages in substantial litigation, regularly intervenes in agency proceedings, and publishes numerous reports and consumer guides.

Center for Concerned Engineering. The center is a spin-off of the Center for Auto Safety. [27] According to the building directory, the two groups share offices in Suite 1223 at 1346 Connecticut Avenue, N.W., Washington, D.C. [28] However, the director of the Center for Concerned Engineering, Ralf Hotchkiss, no longer works out of that office. As we've noted, Hotchkiss co-authored *The Lemon Book: What to Do with Your Bad Car* [29] with Mr. Nader and Lowell Dodge. Mr. Hotchkiss also currently serves as a director of the Disability Rights Center.

The Center for Concerned Engineering provides technical services to government agencies and other groups. It also develops new designs for technological devices used by disabled persons.

The Clean Water Action Project, Inc. CWAP began as a Nader task force on water pollution and was "spun off."[30] Mr. Nader served as a director of CWAP and D.C. registered agent from CWAP's inception until August 21, 1979. According to a CWAP spokesperson, Mr. Nader resigned his positions because of his "lack of time" and the fact that his "services were no longer needed."[31] CWAP still maintains "irregular but also habitual contact" with Nader-controlled organizations.

The president of CWAP, David Zwick, is the author of *Water Wasteland* and co-author of *Who Runs Congress*—books issued under the Nader imprimature. Mark Green, former director of Public Citizen's Congress Watch and Americans Concerned About Corporate Power, serves as Secretary of CWAP, and was one of its incorporators.[32] CWAP receives grants from Public Citizen in 1973 and 1975.

CWAP's goals are the preservation and protection of water resources. In the past, the organization has promoted these goals through lobbying and advocacy in the Congress. More recently, however, it has become increasingly interested in promoting "grass roots" activity.

National Public Interest Research Group (PIRG) Clearinghouse. Mr. Nader personally funded the National PIRG Clearinghouse when it was incorporated in 1974.[33] Donald Ross was its first director. Mr. Ross was previously director of Citizen Action Group, and co-authored with Mr. Nader the PIRG organizing manual, entitled *Action for a Change.*[34] Mr. Ross is now Director of the New York PIRG branch.

The National PIRG Clearinghouse received a grant from the Center for Study of Responsive Law in 1978.

The principal function of this organization is to act as a national coordinating office for the network of state PIRGs.

The Clearinghouse for Professional Responsibility, Inc. Mr. Nader was an initial director of the Clearinghouse for Professional Responsibility, Inc. Peter Petkas, a legal and business advisor to Mr. Nader at the time,[35] was also an initial director and incorporator of the Clearinghouse.

The Clearinghouse was formed in 1971 to encourage professionals to report products and activities that threaten safety or health. The group attempted to carry out this purpose through publicity, speeches, and contacts with professional organizations. It has been defunct or inactive since 1973.

Retired Professional Action Group. Mr. Nader was one of the initial directors of the Retired Professional Action Group. RPAG was wholly funded by Public Citizen, Inc.[36] The group was formed specifically to deal with the problems of the elderly. It merged with the Gray Panthers in 1973.

Congress Project. Mr. Nader personally funded the Project, which he initiated in late 1971. The total cost of the Project was approximately $180,000 to $200,000.[37] The Project was organized to conduct a study of the intricate workings of the Congress. The Project published several reports and a book entitled *Who Runs Congress?*

Citizen Action Group. The now defunct Citizen Action Group was wholly funded by and operated as a subgroup of Public Citizen, Inc.[38] It was formed to build and train public-interest advocacy groups at the state and local levels. CAG helped organize PIRGs in several states.

Capitol Hill News Service. The News Service was "set up" by Mr. Nader.[39] It was almost entirely supported by grants from Public Citizen and had a budget totaling more than $230,000 in 1974–76.[40] The News Service was organized for the purpose of providing small-town newspapers with consumer-oriented news about the activities of local congressmen. It was dissolved in 1978.

Congress Probe. The Probe published a weekly newsletter of the same name about events in Congress. It shared Suite 415 at 1346 Connecticut Avenue N.W., Washington, D.C., with the Nader-controlled Public Interest Research Group. Congress Probe published its final newsletter in June, 1980, and is now defunct.

Residential Utility Citizen Action Group. RUCAG was initiated by Mr. Nader in 1977 in Washington, D.C. It sought to protect "consumer interests" in residential utility issues. RUCAG became defunct in 1979. RUCAG's successor is the Citizens Utility Board project of the Center for Study of Responsive Law.

Consumers Union of the U.S., Inc. Mr. Nader served as a director of Consumers Union from the end of 1967 until late 1975.[41] He was instrumental in the creation of the group's Washington office. Mr. Nader resigned from his position because, he said, "I can better use the ten days a year, which would be spent on CU matters, in other pursuits within the consumer-movement—more broadly defined."[42] Clarence Ditlow

III, a former employee of Public Citizen and the current director of the Center for Auto Safety, also once served as a director of Consumer's Union.

CU provides information to consumers regarding various goods and services in the marketplace. It also publishes a monthly magazine, *Consumer Reports.*

Consumer Complaint Research Center. The Center was a three-year study funded by the Carnegie Corporation of New York in cooperation with the Center for Study of Responsive Law. The purpose of the study was to analyze consumer complaint procedures used in the public and private sectors. In some instances, the Center made recommendations for instituting different methods. Mr. Nader's sister, Mrs. Laura Nader Milleron, served as chairperson of the CCRC's Advisory Board.

Center for Women Policy Studies. The Center was organized in 1972 with "seed money" from Public Citizen, Inc.[43] In addition, "office space was provided at [the Center's] inception by Mr. Nader."[44] The Center is located at 2000 P Street N.W., Washington, D.C.—an address that was common to several other public interest groups including Public Citizen.[45]

The Center conducts research on legal and economic issues affecting women and is currently working on two projects concerning violence in the home.

Connecticut Citizen Action Group. CCAG was organized with the assistance of the Citizen Action Group. It received grants from Public Citizen in 1972 and 1973 that totaled $35,000. Martin Rogol, a former director of CCAG, is also a director of the Aviation Consumer Action Project. Reuben B. Robertson III, a close associate of Mr. Nader,[46] was a director of CCAG in 1977 and 1978. Other Nader associates who have been connected with CCAG over the years include Peter Petkas (secretary, 1973), Harvy Jester (bookkeeper, 1971-73), and Donald K. Ross (president/director/treasurer, 1972). CCAG engages in lobbying activities on a broad range of issues before the Connecticut state legislature.

Connecticut Citizen Research Group. The Group received grants from the Nader-controlled Center for Study of Responsive Law in 1972 and Public Citizen in 1973. The Rosewater Foundation also funded CCRG in 1974, the same year Rosewater received a grant from the Center for Study of Responsive Law.

As of 1978, Marc Caplan was the executive director of CCRG. Mr. Caplan also once served as executive director of the Connecticut Citizen Action Group. Miles Rapoport has since replaced Mr. Caplan as executive director of CCRG as well as director of Connecticut Citizen Action Group.

According to documents filed with the State of Connecticut, CCRG spent all of its money conducting research on environmental and product safety issues.

California Citizen Action Group. The Group was formed, like its Connecticut counterpart, with the guidance of the Citizen Action Group.[47] Roy Alper, a former director of the California CAG, has also served as a director of both the National Consumer Resource Center (now the National Center for Consumers of Legal Services and the Consumer Federation of America).

Ohio Public Interest Action Group, Inc. "During its first year, OPIAG was directed by Ralph Nader and members of the Washington, D.C. PIRG."[48] OPIAG received a grant from Public Citizen in 1973. OPIAG has since closed out its file with the Ohio Charitable Foundations Section.[49]

Gray Panthers and Gray Panthers Project Fund. The Retired Professional Action Group, once wholly funded by Public Citizen, Inc., merged with the National Gray Panthers and Gray Panthers Project Fund in December, 1975.[50] Public Citizen had contributed $12,500 to the Gray Panthers in 1974.

National Gray Panthers and the Gray Panthers Project Fund are virtually identical groups, since "control of each organization is vested in the same elected and appointed individuals and the organizations are under common management."[51]

The consolidated organizations are primarily involved with issues affecting the elderly, such as age discrimination, health care, Social Security, and transportation.

Fund for Investigative Journalism, Inc. The Fund received a grant of $1,500 from the Center for Study of Responsive Law in 1974. The Fund makes grants to writers and reporters who use the funds to investigate corruption in public and private institutions.

The Southwest Research and Information Center. The Center received a $3,000 grant from the Center for Study of Responsive Law in 1975.[52] It currently conducts technical and legal research on environmental and energy issues in the Southwest.

Black Affairs Council, Inc. The Black Affairs Council of Philadelphia, Pennsylvania, received a grant of

$1,000 from the Center for Study of Responsive Law in 1972.[53] The organization is currently inactive.

Small Claims Study Group. The Group was partially funded by Public Citizen in 1972, receiving a total of $9,500.[54] The organization is presently defunct.

The Legal Services Reporter. The Reporter received a grant of $2,500 from Public Citizen in 1973.[55] No current information is available on the Reporter.

For the People. For the People, of Huntington Woods, Michigan, received a grant of $2,000 from Public Citizen in 1974.[56] The organization is now defunct.

D.C. D.E.S. The organization received a grant of $250 from the Center for Study of Responsive Law in 1978.[57] D.C. D.E.S. was formed in response to the recent controversy concerning Diethylstibestrol. The organization publishes a newsletter and testifies before the Food and Drug Administration.

Project on Corporate Responsibility (Campaign GM). The Project was aimed at the upper echelons of General Motors Corp.'s management. Its ultimate objective was to elect members to GM's Board of Directors. The group did not succeed.

The group was organized by two lawyers, Geoffrey Cowan and Philip W. Moore III. They met on September 29, 1969, with Mr. Nader, who "gave them ideas for resolutions, identified issues, provided lists of people to approach for help."[58] On February 7, 1970, Mr. Nader held a press conference with Messrs. Cowan and Moore to launch the Project. "This event," wrote

Nader biographer Charles McCarry, "gave birth to the enduring suspicion, which is not altogether unjustified, that Campaign GM is, in Cowan's phrase, 'a front for Ralph Nader.'"[59] Mr. Nader declined, however, to speak at a Detroit rally for the Project in May, 1970. Robert Townsend, a major contributor (via Rosewater Foundation) to Mr. Nader's Public Safety Research Institute, instead served as the rally's principal speaker.

Project directors Messrs. Cowan and Moore subsequently disassociated themselves from Mr. Nader.[60] The project's name was changed to the "Center on Corporate Responsibility" in 1972.

Professional Drivers Council for Safety and Health. The Council was established with a grant from Public Citizen.[61] The organization was created to work for the unionization of truck drivers. Capital Legal Foundation was unable to gain further information on the Council's activities because the director refused to be interviewed.

Public Equity Corporation. Beverly C. Moore, Jr., formerly a staff attorney with the Nader-controlled Corporate Accountability Research Group, was an initial board member of the Public Equity Corporation. James S. Turner was also a member of the Board. Mr. Turner was once an associate of the Nader-controlled Center for Study of Responsive Law and is author of *The Chemical Feast,* the Nader study group report on food protection and the Food and Drug Administration.[62]

The Corporation withdrew its registration statement from the Securities and Exchange Commission in 1976, less than two years after its incorporation.

The organization was established to engage in litigation and research, and served as a clearinghouse for attorneys engaged in consumer litigation. It is no longer active.

The Press Information Center. The Center was established by Mr. Nader in cooperation with the National Press Club.[63] Its function was to file suits on behalf of journalists under the Freedom of Information Act.

Professionals for Auto Safety, Inc. It was formed as a spin-off of the Center for Auto Safety.[64] Lowell Dodge, then executive director of the Center for Auto Safety, was one of the incorporators and initial directors of Professionals for Auto Safety. The Center studies and evaluates federal legislation and agency regulations concerning motor vehicle safety.

Consumer Federation of America. Marc Caplan, formerly executive director of the Consumer Federation and the Connecticut Citizen Action Group, has sat on the board of the Federation.[65] Roy Alper, another former director of the Consumer Federation, has also served as a director of the California Citizen Action Group and the National Consumer Resource Center.

CFA is a lobbying organization that advances a pro-consumer policy before Congress, regulatory agencies, the executive branch, and the courts. Its funding primarily comes from the 200 organizations that comprise its membership.

Maryland PIRG. The Maryland PIRG branch received a $1,500 grant from the Rosewater Foundation in 1975, the same year that Rosewater received a $5,000 grant from Mr. Nader's Center for Study of Responsive Law. The organization's activities primarily focus on research and lobbying at the state level on a wide variety of issues.

Accountants for the Public Interest. It received grants from the Rosewater Foundation in 1976, 1977, and 1978. The organization provides independent accounting analysis to various public interest organizations.

Citizen Action Fund. Edward Greensfelder was an incorporator, initial director, and initial registered agent for the Citizen Action Fund. He was also an incorporator, initial director, registered agent, and secretary of the Fund for Constitutional Government. He presently serves as an attorney for the Fund for Constitutional Government.

The Articles of Incorporation of the Citizen Action Fund state that it may engage in such activities as "are consistent with the objectives of Public Citizen . . . and Consumer Federation of America." This includes raising funds for other "public interest" organizations, engaging in research, and presenting reports to the Congress and the Executive Branch.

CONCLUSIONS

The preceding survey demonstrates that Mr. Nader and some of his network groups have or had substantial ties to nearly 50 ancillary organizations in the consumer and "public interest" fields. Nader and his network groups often took an active role in the genesis of many of these other organizations, such as providing funding for the Disability Rights Center, Pension Rights Center, National PIRG Clearinghouse, and the Center for Women's Policy Studies. Mr. Nader served as a founding or initial director for others such as the Clearinghouse for Professional Responsibility and Retired Professional Action Group. In still other instances, network groups helped organize related groups such as Consumers Opposed to Inflation in the Necessities, Center for Auto Safety, Fund for Constitutional Government, New York PIRG, and the Citizen Action Group.

With respect to other groups, the Nader network's input was more limited. While it may not have played a role in the establishment of these organizations, the network or Mr. Nader provided financial or other forms of support.

The relationships outlined in this chapter also illuminate the evolution of part of the "public interest" movement in the United States. Mr. Nader, the network, or Nader associates have at some point been affiliated with many of these related groups—whether by virtue of funding, organizational assistance, or program support. On several occasions, Mr. Nader helped promote a group and then formally disassociated himself from it. Such was the case with the Public Interest Research Groups, the Center for Auto Safety, and the Clean Water Action Project, to name just a few of the Nader "spin-off" groups.

On the other hand, as Mr. Nader shifted his strategy from research to lobbying, his affiliation with other groups became more discernible, such as with Public Citizen. Similarly, the activity and prominence of some groups grew—for example, Public Citizen—while others diminished—for example, the Center for Auto Safety. Mike Horrocks, director of Public Citizen's Visitors Center, described this "spin-off" pattern as "an evolutionary process which occurred naturally as certain groups became so active and so big that they became groups in their own right."[66]

The "spin-off" pattern may well be attributable to "evolutionary" processes, but it also exhibits other distinctive features that raise doubt about so simple an

70

appraisal. For instance, many of the "spin-off" groups are limited to specialized areas of interest, such as constituency advocacy by the Gray Panthers or local organizing by the PIRG branches. Many are single-issue organizations.

The limited aims of these groups helps explain why Mr. Nader severed, or at least stretched, many of his ties with these organizations. His primary interest is to see these groups organized and funded adequately at the start. After that he prefers to return to more broad "public interest" issues. Consumers Union of the United States is an example. As we noted, Mr. Nader said he resigned from the group in 1975 because "I can better use the ten days a year, which would be spent on CU matters, in other pursuits within the consumer movement—more broadly defined."[67]

By associating with multi-issue organizations rather than single-issue groups, Mr. Nader is free to decide on an *ad hoc* basis his agenda for "public interest" action. Correspondingly, since the boundaries of Mr. Nader's activities are in theory unlimited, he is able to depict his work as an all-encompassing defense of the interests of the American public. As long as the scope of Mr. Nader's interests remains broadly defined, it is difficult to assess his claim to represent the "public interest." On the other hand, if Mr. Nader were linked only to specific issues and interests—as are a majority of the ancillary organizations—he could no longer claim easily that he worked in the "public interest." Rather, Mr. Nader would become just another "special interest" lobbyist.

(For more details on these ancillary groups, refer to Appendix D.)

NOTES

1. Statement by Roger Hickey, COIN Director—phone conversation, 7/3/80.

2. "Business-caused Inflation," *Congressional Quarterly,* 1/2/79, p. 89.

3. Statement by Roger Hickey, COIN Director—phone conversation, 7/3/80.

4. John Rees, "Ralph Nader, Ripoff Artist," *The Review of the NEWS,* 8/29/79, p. 43.

5. Lois G. Wark, "Consumer Report/Nader campaigns for funds to expand activities of his consumer action complex," *National Journal,* 9/18/71, p. 1909.

6. Form 990 filed by Monsour Medical Foundation with the IRS in 1976.

7. Barbara O'Reilley, "Nader Series," written for Gannett News Service, 3/29/79.

8. Barbara O'Reilley, "Nader Series," written for Gannett News Service, 3/29/79.

9. Rosewater's Form 990-PF filed with the IRS in 1974.

10. CSRL's Form 990 filed with the IRS in 1975.

11. CSRL's Form 990 filed with the IRS in 1976.

12. Rosewater's Form 990-PF filed with the IRS in 1977.

13. Rosewater's Form 990-PF filed with the IRS in 1973.

14. Rosewater's Form 990-PF filed with the IRS in 1974.

15. Constance Holden, "Public Interest: New Group Seeks Redefinition of Scientists' Role," in *Science,* Vol. 173, 7/9/71. Confirmed by Tish Brewster, Assistant Director of CSPI—phone conversation, 7/3/80.

16. As of our visit on May 23, 1980.

17. Statement by Faith Little of the Center—phone conversation, 7/2/80.

18. David Sanford, *Me & Ralph* (New Republic Book Company, Washington, D.C.) 1976, p. 39.

19. Grossman, New York, 1971.

20. Lois G. Wark, "Consumer Report/Nader campaigns for funds to expand activities of his consumer action complex," *National Journal*, 9/18/71, p. 1909.

21. Mr. Robertson first worked for Mr. Nader as a consultant for the Center for Study of Responsive Law, beginning in 1969. Since then, he has held positions with many Nader-connected organizations, including Public Citizen's Litigation Group, the Aviation Consumer Action Project, and the Connecticut Citizen Action Group.

22. Statement by Faith Little of the Center—phone conversation, 7/2/80.

23. Ibid.

24. Theodore Jacqueney, "Washington Pressures/Nader network switches focus to legal action, congressional lobbying," *National Journal*, 6/9/73, p. 845.

25. See detailed discussion of PIRGs in Chapter 2.

26. Grossman, New York, 1971.

27. Lois G. Wark, "Consumer Report/Nader campaigns for funds to expand activities of his consumer action complex," *National Journal*, 9/18/71, p. 1909.

28. We checked the Building Director on 7/1/80.

29. Grossman, New York, 1971.

30. Statement by Gary Steinberg, Canvas Director of CWAP's D.C. area public outreach program—phone conversation, 6/25/80.

31. Ibid.

32. Ibid.

33. Susan Gross, "The Nader Network," *Business and Society Review,* vol. 13 (1975), p. 6.

34. Grossman, New York, 1971. Rev. ed., 1972.

35. Barbara O'Reilley, "Nader Series," written for Gannett News Service, 3/29/80.

36. Theodore Jacqueney, "Washington Pressures/Nader network switches focus to legal action, congressional lobbying," *National Journal,* 6/9/73, p. 846. Annual reports from Public Citizen attached to the affidavit of Sidney Wolfe, M.D., Director of Public Citizen's Health Research Group—9/9/77, in connection with *Health Research Group* v. *Kennedy,* 9ELR 20183 (D.D.C. March 13, 1979). No. 77-0734.

37. Mary Russell, "Nader Takes on Congress," *Washington Post,* 10/1/72.

38. Theodore Jacqueney, "Washington Pressures/Nader network switches focus to legal action, congressional lobbying," *National Journal,* 6/9/73, p. 846. Annual reports from Public Citizen attached to the affidavit of Sidney Wolfe, M.D., Director of Public Citizen's Health Research Group—9/9/77, in connection with *Health Research Group* v. *Kennedy,* 9ELR 20183 (D.D.C. March 13, 1979), No. 77-0734.

39. Susan Gross, "The Nader Network," *Business and Society Review,* Vol. 13 (1975), p. 13.

40. Public Citizen's annual reports, attached to affidavit of Sidney Wolfe, M.D. (Director of Public Citizen's Health Research Group), on September 9, 1977, in *Health Research Group* v. *Kennedy* (9ELR 20183, D.D.C. March 13, 1979). Susan Gross, "The Nader Network," *Business and Society Review,* Vol. 13 (1975), p. 13.

41. Statement by David Berliner, Associate Director of Consumers Union—phone conversation, 6/30/80.

42. Letter from Nader to Consumers Union, in *Consumer Reports* (published by Consumers Union), September, 1975, p. 525.

43. Statement by Jane Chapman, Executive Director of the Center for Women Policy Studies—phone conversation, 6/26/80.

44. Statement by Carolyn Moore of the Center for Women Policy Studies—phone conversation, 6/26/80.

45. Namely: COIN, Health Research Group, Public Citizen Litigation Group, Public Citizen, Freedom of Information Group, Public CitiConsumers Union—phone conversation, 6/30/80.

46. Mr. Robertson worked with Nader-connected groups for ten years, beginning in 1969 as a consultant for the Center for Study of Responsive Law. He has since held positions with Public Citizen's Litigation Group, the Aviation Consumer Action Project, and the Center for Auto Safety, as well.

47. Susan Gross, "The Nader Network," *Business and Society Review*, Vol. 13 (1975), p. 11.

48. Ralph Nader and Donald Ross, *Action for a Change* (New York: Grossman, 1971). Revised edition 1972, p. 144.

49. Statement by Douglas Andrews of the Ohio Charitable Foundations Section—phone conversation, 6/4/80.

50. Statement by Jonathan Glassman, Gray Panther National Coordinator—phone conversation, 8/14/80.

51. "A Note to recent unaudited combined financial statements for National Gray Panthers and Gray Panthers Project Fund," quoted by the National Information Bureau in their report on Gray Panthers Project Fund issued March 17, 1980.

52. Form 990 filed by Center for Study of Responsive Law with the IRS in 1976.

53. Form 990 filed by Center for Study of Responsive Law with the IRS in 1973.

54. Form 990 filed by Public Citizen, Inc. with the IRS in 1973.

55. Form 990 filed by Public Citizen, Inc. with the IRS in 1974.

56. Form 990 filed by Public Citizen, Inc. with the IRS in 1975.

57. Form 990 filed by the Center for Study of Responsive Law with the IRS in 1979.

58. Charles McCarry, *Citizen Nader* (New York: Saturday Review Press, 1972), p. 223.

59. Ibid.

60. Ibid at p. 224.

61. Susan Gross, "The Nader Network," *Business and Society Review,* vol. 13 (1975), p. 9.

62. Grossman, New York, 1970.

63. Theodore Jacqueney, "Washington Pressures/Nader network switches focus to legal action, congressional lobbying," *National Journal,* 6/9/73, p. 843.

64. Lois G. Wark, "Consumer Report/Nader campaigns for funds to expand activities of his consumer action complex," *National Journal,* 9/18/71, p. 1909.

65. According to its Registration Statement filed on 1/1/78 with the State of Connecticut.

66. Interview, June, 5, 1980.

67. Letter from Nader to Consumers Union, in *Consumer Reports* (published by Consumers Union), Sept. 1975, p. 525.

Chapter 5
Network Finances

The large number and broad scope and activities of the Nader network of organizations give rise to the questions: How are they financed? Do these groups operate hand-to-mouth? Or are they, in fact, well-endowed with hefty financial coffers?

In response to inquiries by the Capital Legal Foundation, the Nader network organizations disclosed little about their finances. Moreover, Capital's ability to acquire financial information was restricted by its research methodology which, for instance, ruled out surreptitious investigation. (For more on research techniques, see Appendix A.)

As a result, Capital's study relied almost entirely on publicly available documents filed with the Internal Revenue Service. Most network organizations are required to file an IRS Form 990, "Return of Organization Exempt from Income Tax." The form requires statements of gross contributions and income received, total expenditures, grants made, and net worth. In addition, it requires a list of the organization's governing bodies.

Organizations applying for federal tax exemption are also required to file an IRS Form 1023, or a similar

"Exemption Application," which requests further information about a group's purposes, projects, trust agreements, and articles of incorporation. All of these documents are public information within the meaning of the Freedom of Information Act, 5 U.S.C., Section 552, as amended.

FACTS

Because of the difficulty of obtaining financial data from the network organizations and due to considerations of time and expense, the Capital Legal Foundation limited its financial investigation to six groups: Public Citizen, Inc. (along with its subgroups), Center for the Study of Responsive Law, Aviation Consumer Action Project, National Citizens Committee for Broadcasting, Public Safety Research Institute, and Safety Systems Foundation.

The six organizations had aggregate gross receipts of about $1.9 million in 1978,[1] the year for which Capital has the most reliable and complete information. (The IRS defines gross receipts as the sum of gross sales and receipts plus gross dues and assessments from members and affiliates, plus gross contributions, income, gifts, grants, and other receipts.)

This $1.9 million figure can be broken down between gross income and total contributions, grants, and gifts. Total gross income for the six groups in 1978 was $524,166.[2] (Gross income is defined by the IRS as gross sales and receipts, less cost or other basis and sales expenses of assets sold. This definition includes program-related income such as government program service fees, client fees, sale of merchandise, booklets, subscriptions and even court-awarded attorney's fees. It also encompasses interest, gain or loss on sale of securities, rental income, royalties, and honoraria.) Of the total gross income, the most accrued from Public Citizen, with $353,861, and Center for the Study of Responsive Law, $109,805.[3]

Aggregate contributions, gifts and grants—apart from gross income—totaled about $1.35 million in 1978 for the six groups.[4] The prime recipient was Public Citizen, which received about $1 million.[5]

Total expenditures for the six groups was about $1.61 million in 1978,[6] or about $300,000 less than their gross receipts for that year. (Total expenditures are defined as expenses incurred in generating gross income, contributions and grants made, fund-raising costs, salaries, supplies, telephone service, rent, printing and publications costs, travel expenses, awards, and other program-related expenses.) Public Citizen spent $243,979 of the total for fund-raising.[7]

Net worth, of course, is one of the most important measurements of an organization's financial health. It represents the accumulation of total wealth, or the excess of receipts over expenditure. The aggregate net worth of the six organizations was almost *$3.4 million* in 1978.[8]

The preceding survey represents a general financial overview of the six network organizations. The next portion of this chapter examines the finances of specific groups in greater detail. It also tries to highlight the evolution of funding patterns, some financial interrelationships between the groups, and recent trends in income and expenses.

Public Citizen, Inc. Public Citizen is one of the network's most active and well-funded organizations. It was established in 1971 to raise funds for Nader programs through direct-mail solicitation,[9] and has been rather successful in its efforts. Mr. Nader controlled

Public Citizen until October 28, 1980, when he resigned as president and treasurer.

Public Citizen has shown a remarkable pattern of growth of its net worth since it was founded. At the beginning of 1972, it had a net worth of $411,419[10] and by the end of that year the figure nearly doubled to $751,997.[11] At the end of 1974, its net worth reached nearly $1.3 million,[12] and at the close of 1978 it stood at $1.52 million.[13] In other words, from 1972 to 1978, Public Citizen had increased its net worth by 267 percent by taking in far more money than it spent. In fact, its financial position was so secure that it was able to purchase an old F.B.I. building in Washington for $1.25 million in cash.[14]

Public Citizen's net worth was not disclosed to contributors in its 1978 annual report or solicitation materials. When queried about this in 1978, Mr. Nader responded that if the public wants to know this information, it can either go to the IRS or derive this figure from the financial data listed in each of the seven annual reports published by Public Citizen and its subgroups.[15]

From its inception in 1971 to the close of the 1978 tax year, Public Citizen generated over $10.2 million in total gross income, $8.8 million of which was derived from contributions, interest, royalties and court settlements.[16] It spent about $7.6 million, of which nearly $2 million (26%) was used for fundraising.[17] The rest, minus accumulated net worth, was used to support activities and programs, including those of other public interest groups, who received $311,000 in grants from Public Citizen.[18] The bulk of these grants ($180,000) was disbursed to the Aviation Consumer Action Project, a network organization that received an average of 78 percent of its support from Public Citizen during 1974 to 1978.[19]

Center for the Study of Responsive Law. Private foundations provide most of the funding for Center for the Study of Responsive Law, one of the oldest Nader organizations. It has reportedly received grants from the Carnegie Corporation of New York, the New York Foundation,[20] the New World Foundation,[21] the Midas International Corporation Foundation,[22] the Wallace Eljaber Foundation,[23] the Field Foundation,[24] and the Stern Fund.[25]

CSRL has followed a similar pattern to that of Public Citizen by setting aside a substantial portion of its annual income to build up its net worth. This pattern is highly unusual for most charitable or tax-exempt organizations around the country. Most of these groups spend donations as quickly as they are received in order to further their stated charitable purposes. These groups do, of course, try to squirrel away some money for lean times, but the use of private donations to accumulate wealth is not a common practice.

In 1969, the first year of operation for CSRL, it received $178,117 in contributions and grants,[26] but it spent only $63,482[27] — or less than 36 percent of its receipts. In 1972, CSRL had gross receipts of $388,000 and disbursed $258,000[28] — or less than 67 percent. This relationship between revenues and expenditures continued through 1978, with the percentage of spending of receipts ranging from 50 percent to a high of 72 percent.[29]

CSRL's net worth was $176,511 at the end of 1970.[30] By the end of 1978, its net worth had increased seven-fold to $1.29 million.[31] Thus, CSRL, a trust of which Mr. Nader is managing trustee, has amassed a sizable tax-exempt fortune by spending far less of the tax-deductible contributions than it received.

Aviation Consumer Action Project. Formed in 1971,

the Project was granted tax-exempt status in 1975. Public Citizen was almost the sole contributor to ACAP in 1974 and 1975, providing 96 percent and 95 percent of total contributions in those years respectively. Between 1974 and 1978, Public Citizen gave ACAP $146,135, or 78 percent of all contributions.[32] The Project did not report any grants to other organizations from 1974 to 1978. Safety Systems Foundation, another Nader network organization, did make an $8,000 grant to ACAP in 1979.[33]

In response to Capital Legal Foundation's inquiries, spokespersons for Mr. Nader said that ACAP is no longer affiliated with him or Public Citizen, although they acknowledged that Public Citizen had made grants to the Project in the past.[34] However, an ACAP official said that Mr. Nader serves as chairman of the advisory board, upon which ACAP places "strong reliance for advice."[35] Mr. Nader has been "closely involved" with ACAP since its inception, the official added. In addition, a staff attorney with Public Citizen's Litigation group, John Cary Sims, serves as a board member and District of Columbia registered agent of ACAP.

National Citizens Committee for Broadcasting. NCCB was organized in 1972, and Mr. Nader became chairman of its board of directors in October, 1978.[36]

It receives most of its contributions from foundations and wealthy individuals. In 1978, over 65 percent of its total contributions came from five contributors: General Foods Corp., Stewart R. Mott, The Rockefeller Family Fund, the North Shore Unitarian Society, and Dr. Thomas Radecli.[37] NCCB's remaining income comes from various contributions of less than $5,000 each.

Large contributions from a relatively small

number of contributors have been the norm for NCCB. During the six fiscal years it has filed returns with the IRS, the Committee reported almost $2.1 million in total income, of which contributions accounted for $999,510. Eighteen contributors accounted for at least 61 percent of this contribution total.[38]

Reflective of this relatively small base of financial support, National Citizens Committee for Broadcasting's income pattern has been erratic. During the first six months of its operation, the Committee reported gross receipts of $86,982[39] and spent a mere $36,354.[40] In tax year 1974 (July 1974-June 1975), its income dipped to $63,344,[41] but increased to almost $400,000 during the period July 1976-June 1977.[42] After that year, however, National Citizens Committee for Broadcasting's annual income again was on the decline.[43]

The Committee reported a negative net worth of $33,646 at the end of 1977.[44] In 1978, NCCB received $151,495 in grants, contributions and other income,[45] but spent only $92,858. This left the organization with a net worth of $24,991.[46]

Public Safety Research Institute. PSRI is a private foundation controlled by Mr. Nader, who serves as president and treasurer. It was organized in 1968 and began filing financial reports in 1969.

Mr. Nader started PSRI as a Delaware corporation[47] in 1968 with $150,000 in seed money from two businessmen, Robert Townsend and Donald Petrie.[48] PSRI reported $150,000 in contributions (the amount received from Townsend and Petrie) and $5,874 in interest income on its 1969 tax return.[49] The organization made no grants in 1969 and closed its books with a net worth of $152,946.[50] PSRI incurred miscellaneous expenses of $254 in 1969.[51]

In 1970, PSRI ventured into the stock market and used its tax-exempt dollars to make several speculative market transactions, including high-risk "short sales." A short sale is a speculative venture in which the investor literally "borrows" stock, sells it, and bets that the price of the stock will go down before he has to put his own money into it and finalize the transaction. While affording the chance of making a quick profit, short sales are extremely risky and are usually undertaken only by sophisticated investors.

Despite the risk, PSRI engaged in at least 13 short sales in 1970.[52] For example, on February 24, 1970, PSRI sold 300 shares of Kentucky Fried Chicken stock for $11,270.[53] On April 10, 1970, the organization repurchased the stock for $9,102, thereby realizing a $2,168 gain in just over a month.[54] On May 6, 1970, PSRI realized a $345 gain in one day on an $8,237 investment when it sold short 100 shares of Polaroid, Inc.[55]

Not all of PSRI's short-selling activity ended on a profitable note. The organization absorbed a $4,000 loss on an investment of $15,000 in Narcor, Inc., stock.[56] Yet another short-sale loser for PSRI was its investment in Carrier Corporation stock. On August 28, 1970, PSRI sold 200 shares of Carrier stock for $6,205. The next day it repurchased the stock, at a $380 loss.[57]

Some of PSRI's stock market activity did not involve short-selling. The organization consummated several more conventional, "long" transactions. For example, on September 4, 1970, PSRI bought 200 shares of Monsanto Corporation for $7,565.[58] One month later PSRI sold the stock at a loss of $1,012. On October 16, PSRI bought 300 shares of Texaco, Inc., an investment of $10,134.[59] Just two weeks later, the stock was sold for $9,651, a $483 loss. Finally, on January 28, 1970, PSRI bought 200 shares of Buffalo Forge Company stock for $10,288. Two days later the stock was sold for $9,404, an $884 loss in just two days.[60]

The aforementioned examples of PSRI short sales and other stock purchases in 1970 are not exhaustive. PSRI bought and sold stock worth over $750,000 in 1970, and engaged in 67 market transactions. PSRI's total assets were "turned over" in new investments five different times.

To place PSRI's stock-market activity in perspective, it is useful to note PSRI's stated purposes, as expressed in its first tax return (Form 990-A, 1969):

> The trust has *no* business activities but is engaged *solely* in charitable, educational and scientific activities, namely, the sponsoring of research projects and the dissemination of information as well as the making of grants to charities qualified within the meaning of Section 501 (c) (3) of the IRC of 1954.[61] [Emphasis added]

PSRI purchased approximately $19,000 worth of stock in 1969, and collected $150,000 in contributions and grants, yet it made no grants or other disbursements to charitable organizations in that year.[62]

Since the effective date in 1970 of the Tax Reform Act of 1969, which sought to prevent abuses of the tax-exempt charity sections of the Internal Revenue Code by requiring private foundations to distribute a minimum amount of grants in order to maintain tax-exempt status, PSRI has distributed grants each year. Most of the grants have gone to the Center for the Study of Responsive Law.[63] However, PSRI has only distributed the minimum amount necessary to maintain tax-exempt status.[64] Thus, as of 1979, PSRI had disbursed $139,000 in grants, or $11,000 less than the seed money

Mr. Nader used to establish the organization ten years before.

In 1970, PSRI's stock dealings aroused the interest of the IRS, which audited PSRI's 1970 tax return. At the conclusion of the audit, the IRS charged the organization with "churning"—the buying and selling of stock at an excessively rapid rate. Charitable foundations are not generally permitted to engage in "churning" because such activity jeopardizes charitable purposes. According to a Gannett News Service article, PSRI settled with the IRS, rather than go to court, and was assessed and paid a fine.[65]

In the aftermath of the 1970 IRS audit, PSRI has invested primarily in "long" rather than "short" stock transactions. Nevertheless, there remain other PSRI investments which deserve mention.

For example, on August 1, 1973, PSRI bought 300 shares of Allied Chemical stock for $11,164.23.[66] At that time, (1) Allied Chemical was the primary manufacturer of airbags; (2) Ralph Nader was the principal advocate of a proposal requiring that new cars be equipped with airbags; and (3) Mr. Nader was president of PSRI. The next day General Motors announced plans to install air bags in 1974 automobiles as an option. PSRI sold its Allied stock on November 19, 1973, for $12,742.33[67] and realized a tax-free 12 percent gain for a three-and-a-half-month investment.

In 1976, PSRI and Safety Systems Foundation had $17,348 invested in Goodyear Tire and Rubber Co. stock. At the same time, the Center for Auto Safety persuaded the National Highway Traffic Safety Administration (NHTSA) to investigate the Firestone "500" series of steel-belted radials. When the investigation was instigated, the head of NHTSA was Joan Claybrook, former head of Public Citizen's Congress Watch.

The NHTSA investigation eventually resulted in recall of the Firestone tires in November 1978. Firestone stock experienced a decline in value after the recall.[68] PSRI held the Goodyear stock at least until the end of 1978, according to IRS documents.

At the close of 1979, PSRI held nearly $182,000 in cash, checking, savings and other interest-bearing accounts. In addition, it owned $169,698 worth of bonds and government obligations. Its net worth was $340,371.[69]

Safety Systems Foundation. Like PSRI, Safety Systems Foundation is another network organization whose financial dealings merit careful attention. The foundation is directed by Mr. Nader's sister, Laura Nader Milleron, who serves as its trustee. With the possible exception of 1971,[70] Ralph Nader has been nearly the sole contributor to SSF, having contributed at least $190,000 to the organization since its inception in 1966 up until the end of 1979.[71]

SSF reported a net worth of $229,225 at the end of 1979.[72] The organization at that time held $177,687 in savings and other interest-bearing accounts. In addition, it owned $15,661 worth of U.S. government obligations and an additional $35,878 in various corporate stocks.[73]

The stated purpose of Safety Systems is to "engage solely in charitable, educational, and scientific activities, namely the sponsoring of research projects and the dissemination of information as well as the making of grants to charities qualified within the meaning of Section 501 (c) (3) of the IRC of 1954.[74]

Between 1967 and 1969, Safety Systems distributed nothing in grants.[75] In 1970, it has been reported, Joan Claybrook received $200.[76] During the period

1967–1969, Safety Systems Foundation received at least $46,000 in tax-deductible contributions from Mr. Nader.[77]

SSF's grant activity has increased since 1970. But the "charities" which have benefited from SSF's benevolence have primarily been other "public interest" groups. Between 1972 and 1975, it disbursed at least $16,000 in grants to CSRL.[78]

In addition to its charitable activities, SSF was an active trader in the stock market. Over a span of 12 years, it made more than 127 purchases of corporate stocks and bonds, and earned $62,785 in tax-exempt investment income. Most of its market activity occurred during the late 1960s and early 1970s. Between 1969 and the end of 1971, the organization consummated 60 stock transactions—24 in 1969, 16 in 1970, and 20 in 1971. As previously mentioned, both SSF and PSRI purchased Goodyear stock in 1976. SSF held its Goodyear stock at least until the end of 1979.

However, SSF participated in many other stock transactions as well. One notable transaction occurred at the time of the proposed merger of International Telephone and Telegraph Corp. and Hartford Fire Insurance Co. In 1970, these two corporate giants proposed what was then reported as the largest corporate merger in history. In April 1970, Ralph Nader attempted to block the merger by submitting a 50-page brief to the Connecticut Insurance Commissioner, whose approval was required before the merger could be effected.[79]

On May 15, 1970, approximately two and one half weeks after Mr. Nader's well-publicized challenge to the merger, and prior to its approval, SSF invested $7,992 in a short sale of ITT stock. The value of the stock fell, and SSF realized a $700 profit on a six-day investment. SSF closed its short position on May 21, 1970, two days before the Commissioner approved the merger.

A reporter questioned Mr. Nader about the timing of the stock transaction. He replied that it was "mere coincidence" and stated that he had no control over SSF's investment.[80] However, Mr. Nader's sister, Laura Nader Milleron, has been the sole trustee of SSF since its inception, and Mr. Nader has been its sole contributor. In a supplement to SSF's IRS form 1023, which was originally filed on January 26, 1967, and supplemented on April 27, 1967, it was acknowledged that Mr. Nader expressed his willingness to serve in an advisory capacity.

SSF engaged in several other speculative stock transactions in 1970. SSF's stock dealings prompted an IRS audit of the organization. The IRS charged SSF with making investments that "jeopardize charitable purposes." As a result of its investigation, the IRS levied $3,087 in penalty fines against SSF and PSRI. They paid the fines rather than contest them.[81]

CONCLUSIONS

The Nader network's finances are intricate, varied and often obscure. It is clear, nonetheless, that this is no "bedraggled army of the night" living hand-to-mouth. It is, rather, a network of sizable financial assets, a fact these groups do not like to publicize. The Capital Legal Foundation's research revealed that the aggregate net worth of only 6 of the 19 network organizations stood at $3.4 million at the end of 1978 (the latest year for which Capital was able to acquire complete data). The network's coffers were filled by collecting much more money than was spent on the "public interest" cause.

For instance, the Center for the Study of Responsive Law increased its net worth seven-fold between 1970 and 1978 to almost $1.3 million. The Center is a trust under the directorship of Mr. Nader and is one of his oldest organizations. Despite its substantial assets, CSRL did not use much of its wealth to subsidize the activities of its sister—and probably more needy— organizations in the Nader network. Much of its money was instead tucked away for safe-keeping. It is difficult, therefore, to avoid the conclusion that CSRL's primary financial preoccupation is self-aggrandizement.

Public Citizen's net worth is even larger, amounting to $1.5 million at the end of 1978. Unlike CSRL, however, Public Citizen received a measurable amount of direct financial support from the general public, and it did distribute a discernible share of its funds to other "public interest" groups. But it is a telling fact that Public Citizen's financial position was so secure that it was able to purchase the F.B.I. building in Washington for $1.25 million *in cash* in 1979.

Public Citizen has been unwilling to disclose much about its financial strength to the public. In its 1979 annual report to contributors, for example, it did not disclose its beginning-year $1.5 million net worth. When questioned about the omission, Mr. Nader responded that if the public wants to know about such financial data, it can go to the state governments, or refer to each of Public Citizen's annual reports.[82]

Mr. Nader, of course, should have known that the aggregate figures were not included in Public Citizen's 1978 annual report. Moreover, he likely knew that the mechanics of getting information through the IRS are arduous and can take about a year and a half. In short, Mr. Nader's suggestions for obtaining financial information about Public Citizen fall woefully short of reasonable standards of disclosure for any non-profit charity, and stand in sharp contrast to his own demands for more disclosure to the public by corporations and government.

Why would Mr. Nader want to make it so difficult for the public to acquire financial data on his "public interest" groups? There are at least two possible reasons: one is to hide their sizable economic resources from the public eye. The network is fond of portraying itself as impoverished and as battling against a well-financed opposition. These opposing lobbying groups may indeed be well-financed, but the Nader network is by no means impoverished. This revelation would certainly alter the public's impression of the Nader groups. Popular sympathy, not to mention contributions, for the Nader cause might diminish.

Another reason for the financial obfuscation might be to conceal the fact that these organizations take in far more money than they spend. If the general public knew that Nader groups were using donations to increase their own corporate wealth, rather than to finance projects for public benefit, it is at least possible that the stream of foundation contributions and other donations would dry up.

The Capital Legal Foundation found that even when network groups spend their money, it may be just to fund another organization in the network instead of a truly "public interest" project. Two network groups — Aviation Consumer Action Project and the Center for the Study of Responsive Law — receive substantial contributions from other network groups. During 1974 to 1978, Public Citizen made grants totaling over $146,000 to ACAP. The grants represented almost 80 percent of the contributions received by ACAP during the period. In 1979, Public Citizen gave $27,523 to ACAP, which was the only grant made by Public Citizen that year.[83]

CSRL has received substantial contributions from Safety Systems Foundation, whose almost sole source of revenue is Mr. Nader's personal income. In addition, SSF made an $8,000 grant to ACAP in 1979.

As indicated by these interorganizational income transfers, several network groups apparently feel that charity begins at home. This tendency, coupled with the accumulation of substantial wealth by CSRL and Public Citizen, leads to the conclusion that the network groups are preoccupied by a financial concern for self-perpetuation rather than spending money to further the "public good."

The financial data examined by the Capital Legal Foundation admits of several other observations. Only one group, Public Citizen, enjoys any substantial amount of direct financial support from the public. Groups such as Safety Systems Foundation and ACAP receive little direct financial assistance from the public, and depend on interorganizational transfers for the bulk of their funding.

CSRL and the National Citizens Committee for Broadcasting rely on large contributions from a relatively small number of contributors. Public Safety Research Institute relies for its income on interest and dividend payments from its corporate and government bonds and its corporate stock holdings. With the possible exception of 1972, PSRI has not received any contributions from the public since 1969.[84]

PSRI and SSF have also used their tax-exempt dollars to engage in several stock-market transactions and failed to include these activities in the initial Form 990As they filed with the IRS in 1969 and 1970, respectively. In both cases, the groups stated they intended to engage only in charitable, educational, and scientific activities, and making grants to other qualified charities. PSRI specifically represented in its 1969 Form 990A to the IRS that the trust had no business activities. After IRS investigations, both groups settled and agreed to pay fines to the IRS.

In sum, the "public interest" label has been a money-maker for the Nader network. By spending far less than they acquire, these groups have stored away more than a nest egg; they have amassed a small fortune. Nor is the use of these funds always in keeping with traditional non-profit activities. Certainly, "short sales" of stock, in hopes of making a quick profit on speculation, are not typical of the financial propriety that governs the investment activities of most non-profit organizations in the United States.

NOTES

1. This figure was determined by adding together the gross receipts on the 1978 tax returns or annual report of each of the organizations.

2. This figure was determined by adding together the gross incomes reported on the 1978 tax returns and/or annual reports of each of the six groups.

3. Public Citizen's Form 990 (1978). Center for Study of Responsive Law's Form 990 (1978).

4. This figure was determined by adding the contributions, gifts and grants reported on the 1978 tax returns or annual report of each of the six organizations.

5. Public Citizen's Form 990 filed with the IRS for 1978.

6. This figure was determined by adding together the expenditures reported on the 1978 tax returns and/or annual reports filed by each of the six organizations.

7. Public Citizen's Annual Report filed with the New York Department of State in 1978.

8. This figure was determined by adding together the net worth reported on the 1978 tax returns and/or annual reports filed by each of the six organizations.

9. Joseph Lelyveld, "Nader Undaunted by Setbacks to Consumer Drive," *New York Times,* 11/24/75, p. 1.

10. Public Citizen's Form 990 filed with the IRS in 1973.

11. Ibid.

12. Form 990s filed with the IRS in 1974 and 1975.

13. Form 990 filed with the IRS in 1979.

14. Ann Zimmerman, "Nader Pays $1,250,000 Cash for Office Building," *Washingtonian,* June 1980, p. 11.

15. Barbara O'Reilley, "Nader Series," written for the Gannett News Service, 3/29/79.

16. Figures are derived from Form 990s filed with the IRS.

17. Ibid.

18. Ibid.

19. Public Citizen's Form 990s filed with the IRS, 1975-79.

20. Ralph de Toledano, *Hit and Run.* (Arlington House, New Rochelle), 1975, p. 97.

21. Ibid.

22. Ibid. at p. 98.

23. John Rees, "Ralph Nader, Ripoff Artist," *The Review of the News,* 8/29/79, p. 41.

24. Theodore Jacqueney, "Washington Pressures/Nader Network Switches Focus to Legal Action, Congressional Lobbying," *National Journal,* 6/9/73, p. 844.

25. Ibid.

26. Form 990-A filed with the IRS in 1970.

27. Ibid.

28. Form 990 filed with the IRS in 1973.

29. Form 990s filed with the IRS in 1971, 1974, 1975, 1976, 1978, and 1979.

30. Form 990 filed with the IRS in 1971.

31. Form 990 filed with the IRS in 1979.

32. Form 990s filed by Public Citizen and ACAP with the IRS, 1974-79.

33. Form 990 filed by Safety Systems with the IRS in 1980.

34. Mike Horrocks, Director of Public Citizen's Visitor Center— interview, 6/5/80. Emmy Smith, accountant for Public Citizen and Center for Study of Responsive Law—phone conversation, 6/3/80.

35. Statement by Kathy Waldbauer, Administrative Assistant with ACAP—phone conversation, 6/26/80.

36. Statement by Joe Waz, Deputy Director of NCCB—phone conversation, 6/30/80.

37. Form 990 filed with NCCB in 1979.

38. A. Stuart Hanisch ($40,913), William Benton Fund ($50,000), Abelard Foundation ($25,000), North Shore Unitarian Society ($60,000), Rockefeller Family Fund ($35,000), Max and Anna Levinson Foundation ($15,000), John and Markle Foundation ($115,125), American Medical Association ($63,630), Stern Fund ($50,000), J.M. Kaplan Fund ($60,000), Stewart Rawlings Mott ($22,782), Norman Foundation ($17,000), Arca Foundation ($10,000), Laras Fund ($10,000), General Foods Corporation ($20,000), Dr. Thomas Radecli ($8,100), Ottinger Foundation ($5,000), Mrs. Bettina W. Grimson ($5,036).

39. Form 990 filed with the IRS in 1973.

40. Form 990 filed with the IRS in 1978.

41. Form 990s filed with the IRS in 1979 and 1976.

42. Form 990 filed with the IRS in 1977.

43. Form 990 filed with the IRS in 1978.

44. Ibid.

45. Form 990 filed with the IRS in 1979.

46. Ibid.

47. Form 1023 (Exemption Application) filed with the IRS in 1968.

48. Barbara O'Reilley, "Nader Series," written for the Gannett News Service, 3/29/79.

49. Form 990 filed with the IRS in 1970.

50. Ibid.

51. Ibid.

52. PSRIs Form 990 filed with the IRS in 1971.

53. Ibid.

54. Ibid.

55. Ibid.

56. Ibid.

57. Ibid.

58. Ibid.

59. Ibid.

60. Barbara O'Reilley, "Nader Series," written for the Gannett News Service, 3/29/79.

61. Form 990 filed with the IRS in 1970.

62. Form 990 filed with the IRS in 1970.

63. Since 1970 (excluding 1972—IRS return unavailable), PSRI has made $139,100 in grants to other organizations. CSRL has received $56,000, Pension Rights Center has received $47,000 and the Disability Rights Center has received $23,700.

64. Barbara O'Reilley, "Nader Series," written for the Gannett News Service, 3/29/79.

65. Ibid.

66. PSRI's Form 990 filed with the IRS in 1974.

67. Ibid.

68. Barbara O'Reilley, "Nader Series," written for the Gannett News Service, 3/29/79.

69. Form 990-AR filed with the IRS in 1980.

70. We requested but did not receive SSFs Form 990 from the IRS for that year.

71. Figure derived from SSFs Form 990s filed with the IRS for the time period 1966-79.

72. Form 990 P.F. filed with the IRS in 1980.

73. Ibid.

74. Form 990-A filed with the IRS in 1970.

75. Form 990s filed with the IRS 1967-1969.

76. Ibid.

77. Ibid.

78. Form 990s filed with the IRS, 1973-76.

79. Barbara O'Reilley, "Nader Series," written for the Gannett News Service, 3/29/79.

80. Ibid.

81. Ibid.

82. Ibid.

83. Public Citizen's 1979 Annual Report filed with the N.Y. State Department of State.

84. PSRI's Form 990s filed with the IRS, 1970-80.

Chapter 6
Compliance with Law

Most states require organizations that solicit contributions from the public to register as charities and to file annual reports on their activities. The primary purpose is to protect the public from fraudulent solicitation. In addition, these laws provide state officials and the public with pertinent information about the charities' operations and statements of purposes. With these centralized sources about fund-raising, officials can oversee the collection and dispersal of charitable funds within their states, and the information helps the public to determine the worthiness of these causes. In short, these are classic public protection statues similar to the Consumer Protection Act, which Ralph Nader and some network groups supported in Congress in 1978.

State officials take these solicitation laws seriously. Penalties for noncompliance range from a letter directing an organization to comply, to a $5,000 fine and two years in jail for willful violations, to revocation of solicitation privileges. The disclosure requirements apply to *all* charities. The mere fact that a group purports to represent the "general public" or "consumer interests" does not exempt it from the disclosure requirements. All groups are equally subject to the laws.[1]

And all documents filed pursuant to these state statutes are public information.

Since some of the Nader network organizations solicit contributions from the public, the Capital Legal Foundation expected to find a wealth of information about their operations in the public record of disclosure requirements. Upon investigation, however, it discovered otherwise.

FACTS

The Capital Legal Foundation commenced its investigation in the District of Columbia, where several Nader network organizations operate. Public Citizen, Inc., and the National Citizens Committee for Broadcasting, as we've pointed out, for example, have their headquarters in Washington, D.C.

The Business Licensing Branch of the District of Columbia Department of Licenses is responsible for maintaining the records of charitable organizations that are required to register under the District's charitable solicitation statute.[2] (For detailed information on solicitation laws throughout the United States, see Appendix E.)

It may be useful to outline the District of Columbia statute. The D.C. solicitation statute provides that "no person shall solicit in the District of Columbia unless he holds a valid certificate of registration authorizing such solicitation."[3] "Person" is defined as "any individual, firm, partnership, corporation, company, association, society, organization, or other similar representative thereof."[4]

The D.C. statute broadly defines solicitation as ". . . the request, directly or indirectly, for any contribution on the plea or representation that such contribution will or may be used for any charitable purpose, and also means and includes any of the following methods of securing contributions: (1) oral or written request; (2) the distribution, . . . or publishing of any handbill, written advertisement, or publication; . . ."[5] "Solicitation" is deemed "completed when made, whether or not the person making the same receives any contribution . . . ."[6] Regulations promulgated pursuant to the statute provide that a person claiming exemption from the requirements of the Act shall not solicit contributions until that person has filed the required proof of exemption with the Department of Licensing.[7]

Many of Public Citizen's brochures and bulletins, obtained from the Public Citizen Visitors Center, contain requests for contributions.[8] These contribution requests constitute solicitation within the letter of the District of Columbia statute. Public Citizen, Inc., is therefore required to register with the Department of Licensing, or to apply for an exemption from the statute. In either case, the organization's registration or its exemption application must be filed with the Department of Licensing and a certificate granted at least 15 days prior to any solicitation.

However, Joseph Richards, director of the Washington D.C. Business Licensing Branch informed us on June 2, 1980, that Public Citizen, Inc., was not registered as a charitable organization in the District of Columbia. He also said there was no record indicating that Public Citizen had ever applied for an exemption.[9]

We also inquired about the compliance of National Citizens Committee for Broadcasting, which is affiliated with Ralph Nader.[10] NCCB maintains its headquarters and offices in the District of Columbia. Mr. Richards said that to the best of his knowledge and belief NCCB has neither registered with the Business

Licensing Branch nor applied for exemption from the statute at any time since the group's inception in 1972.

We then made inquiries in eight additional jurisdictions where these two network organizations operate: Illinois, Maryland, Massachusetts, Michigan, New Jersey, New York, Ohio, and Pennsylvania. Each of these states has a statute regulating charitable solicitations within the state.

Because of considerations of time and expense, we limited our inquiries in these eight states to two network organizations: Public Citizen, Inc., and National Citizens Committee for Broadcasting. We selected these two organizations because they are both major "public interest" organizations which have discernible, direct ties to Ralph Nader. At the time of our inquiries, Mr. Nader was president and treasurer of Public Citizen, Inc.,[12] and chairman of the board of National Citizens Committee for Broadcasting.[13]

On June 18, 1980, we contacted the state offices responsible for the administration of the charitable solicitation statutes. Public Citizen, Inc., was registered in only four of the eight states—New Jersey, Pennsylvania, Illinois, and New York. National Citizens Committee for Broadcasting was not registered in *any* of the eight jurisdictions. Consequently, we expanded our investigation to encompass all states in the United States.

A telephone survey of all states, conducted from June 23 to 25, 1980, revealed that 33 states, in addition to the District of Columbia, have charitable solicitation statutes. These are: Arkansas, California, Colorado,[14] Connecticut, Florida, Georgia, Hawaii, Illinois, Kansas, Kentucky, Maine, Maryland, Massachusetts, Michigan, Minnesota, Nebraska, New Hampshire, New Jersey, New York, North Carolina, North Dakota, Ohio, Oklahoma, Oregon, Pennsylvania, Rhode Island, South Carolina, South Dakota, Tennessee, Virginia, Washington, West Virginia, and Wisconsin.

In addition to expanding the geographical scope of the compliance survey, we enlarged the subject matter of our inquiry. We requested detailed information on the scope of the various statutes, including: the content of the statutes and regulations, the statute's definition of solicitation; the procedure for exemptions; and enforcement procedures.

We learned that the Public Citizen and NCCB were only registered in a small number of jurisdictions. Public Citizen, Inc., was registered in 6 of the 34 jurisdictions that have charitable solicitation statutes: California, Illinois, Minnesota, New Jersey, New York, and Pennsylvania. In a registration statement submitted to the State of Minnesota on December 27, 1978, Public Citizen stated that it solicits in "all 50 states of the United States." Ralph Nader and Emmy Smith, Nader's accountant, signed the statement.

Public Citizen, Inc., had neither registered nor applied for exemption in eight jurisdictions where the statute requires a charitable organization to either register or file an application for exemption prior to any solicitation. The jurisdictions are: Connecticut, the District of Columbia, Florida, Maine, Maryland, Virginia, South Carolina, and West Virginia. In addition, Public Citizen, Inc. had not registered in 15 other jurisdictions: Arkansas, Georgia, Hawaii, Kansas, Kentucky, Massachusetts, Michigan, Nebraska, New Hampshire, North Dakota, Oklahoma, South Dakota, Tennessee, Washington, and Wisconsin. The charitable solicitation statutes in each of the 15 states require a charitable organization to register prior to any solicitation of funds unless otherwise exempted. None of the exemptions apply to Public Citizen.

The National Citizens Committee for Broadcasting was, at the time of our research, registered only in Minnesota. NCCB filed a registration statement with Minnesota on June 17, 1977, which stated that the group solicits funds in "all states." Executive officer Ted Carpenter and secretary-treasurer Robert Stein signed the statement. Ralph Nader is now on the Board of National Citizens Committee for Broadcasting.

NCCB had neither registered nor applied for exemptions in 10 jurisdictions where the statutes require a charitable organization to make such applications prior to any solicitation. The 10 jurisdictions are: Connecticut, the District of Columbia, Florida, Maine, Maryland, New Jersey, Pennsylvania, South Carolina, Virginia, and West Virginia.

Additionally, NCCB had failed to register in 15 other jurisdictions—Arkansas, Georgia, Hawaii, Kansas, Kentucky, Massachusetts, Michigan, Nebraska, New Hampshire, North Dakota, Oklahoma, South Dakota, Tennessee, Washington, and Wisconsin. The charitable solicitation statutes in each of these states require a charitable organization to register prior to any solicitation unless otherwise exempted.

New York State authorities have investigated the registration of the Center for the Study of Responsive Law (as detailed in Chap. 7). However, we did not include CSRL in the main body of the compliance survey because of a lack of information regarding its solicitation activities and the inconclusiveness of our findings with regard to statutory requirements for trusts. Nonetheless, some discussion of CSRL is warranted.

CSRL is not currently registered in any jurisdiction and has not applied for any exemptions. It had registered in New York in 1972 as the consequence of inquiries by the New York Office of Charities Registration. But CSRL did not file an annual report with the state as the statute required.[15] As a result, the Office of Charities Registration canceled CSRL's registration in 1973 and banned CSRL from further solicitation in New York.[16]

In response to a 1976 request by the Office of Charities Registration that CSRL file back-reports,[17] CSRL sent a letter from its accountant, Harvey Jester, which asserted that CSRL was not required to furnish registration statements because the "Center has not raised funds in New York since 1971, does not presently solicit funds there, nor does it have such plans for the future."[18] The letter further stated that "The Center, by definition, does not solicit funds from the public anywhere in the country. It is a research organization which receives grants for special studies."[19]

New York, however, does not feel bound by CSRL's definition of "solicitation." The state official we interviewed stated that "solicitation" in New York is understood to be implied whenever an organization receives funds from other organizations or persons in the state, regardless of how they receive them.[20] The official indicated that New York is prepared to investigate CSRL's failure to register upon the filing of a complaint.[21]

We believe that the New York Office of Charities Registration is correct in its interpretation of CSRL's registrability. Sufficient doubts exist as to warrant further investigation, and we wholeheartedly endorse any future efforts by the New York charitable authorities.

The New York registration statute is not unique. The statutory language of the Oklahoma and California statutes indicate that if an organization receives contributions from other organizations or persons in the state, the organization must register unless it is otherwise exempt.

CONCLUSIONS

We believe we have documented a pervasive pattern of noncompliance by the subject organizations. The facts we gathered show that: (1) As of time of our survey, Public Citizen was in apparent violation of the charitable solicitation statutes of as many as 23 jurisdictions,[22] and (2) NCCB has apparently not complied with the solicitation laws of 25 jurisdictions.[23] The actual extent of noncompliance may be more substantial because (1) our inquiry was limited to two network organizations; (2) much of the information on which a determination of compliance depends is peculiarly within the possession of the groups, who resist disclosure of the pertinent information; and (3) enforcement mechanisms, which generally require a third-party complaint, are relatively inadequate and easy to circumvent.

Our survey discloses a symbiotic relationship between the shroud of secrecy that envelops network finances and the general lack of compliance with solicitation statutes. So long as the groups continue to withhold pertinent financial information respecting the scope of funding and solicitation, any truly systematic and exhaustive inquiry into compliance is effectively precluded.

Network organizations solicit millions of dollars from public citizens. Few citizens actually know how the money is being spent. So long as the groups ignore laws designed to make such information available to the public, the public will remain in the dark.

On innumerable occasions, Mr. Nader and network organizations have insisted that government and business recognize a duty of disclosure and accountability with respect to matters affecting the public interest. Yet, Mr. Nader and the network groups demonstrate a reprehensible disregard and contempt for the letter and spirit of state disclosure laws. To our mind, the network's failure to comply with these laws constitutes an arrogant abuse of public trust. Why should Public Citizen be accountable to no one? Why does it hypocritically insist on much greater accountability from others? It is repugnant that a group which purports to represent the public interest considers itself above the law.

NOTES

1. Capital Legal Foundation was registered, or was in the process of registering in every state that requires registration.

2. D.C. Code Section 2-2101 et seq. (1973).

3. Ibid.

4. Ibid.

5. Ibid.

6. Ibid.

7. Ibid.; 5 VDCCR 11.1 (1970).

8. For example, the back page of Public Citizen's 1979 annual report has a contribution form attached.

9. Phone conversation with Joseph Richards, Director of D.C. Business Licensing Branch, 6/2/80.

10. See Chapter 4 for a detailed description of the nature of the connection between Nader and NCCB.

11. Phone conversation with Joseph Richards, 6/2/80.

12. Nader has since resigned from these positions. See "Ralph Nader Resigns from Consumer Post," *Washington Post,* 10/28/80.

13. Form 990 filed with the IRS in 1980.

14. Colorado's statute does not require a charitable organization to register with the state but it does contain provisions relating to conduct of such organizations. Phone conversation with Mr. Stephan Caplan of Colorado's Office of the Attorney General on June 24, 1980.

15. Letter to CSRL from N.Y. Bureau of Charitable and Proprietary Organizations, 4/25/73.

16. Letter to CSRL from N.Y. Bureau of Charitable and Proprietary Organizations, 10/16/73.

17. Letter to CSRL from N.Y. Bureau of Charitable and Proprietary Organizations, 1/5/76.

18. Letter from CSRL to N.Y. Bureau of Charitable and Proprietary Organizations, 1/9/76.

19. Ibid.

20. Phone conversation with Mr. Cozzens of the New York Office of Charities Registration, 7/12/80.

21. Ibid.

22. Arkansas, Connecticut, District of Columbia, Florida, Georgia, Hawaii, Kansas, Kentucky, Maine, Maryland, Massachusetts, Michigan, Nebraska, New Hampshire, North Dakota, Oklahoma, South Carolina, South Dakota, Tennessee, Virginia, Washington, West Virginia, Wisconsin.

23. Arkansas, Connecticut, District of Columbia, Florida, Georgia, Hawaii, Kansas, Kentucky, Maine, Maryland, Massachusetts, Michigan, Nebraska, New Hampshire, New Jersey, North Dakota, Oklahoma, Pennsylvania, South Carolina, South Dakota, Tennessee, Virginia, Washington, West Virginia, Wisconsin.

Chapter 7
Nader's Accountability

Several public authorities and quasi-public bodies have experienced difficulty obtaining information from Ralph Nader's network of organizations. Even Congress has on occasion encountered difficulties. The Capital Legal Foundation, in the course of its investigation of the network, also faced similar problems in gathering information. These instances gave rise to the question of whether the network fails generally to respond to reasonable outside inquiries.

FACTS

An illustrative case involves the Center for the Study of Responsive Law and the difficulties experienced by New York State authorities. In 1972 CSRL registered as a charitable organization qualified to solicit funds in New York. The New York State Bureau of Charitable and Proprietary Organizations acknowledged receipt of the registration statement and, in a letter dated September 21, 1972, requested CSRL to file a copy of its 1971 annual report, as required by state law.[1] The Bureau specifically requested the Center to file its report by March 2, 1973.[2]

By April 25, 1973, state officials had yet to receive a copy of the Center's annual report. The Bureau then advised CSRL that it would cancel the Center's charitable organization registration if its annual report was not filed by May 10, 1973.[3] On October 16, 1973, the Bureau "canceled" the Center's registration because of failure to file the annual report by the required date. It advised the Center to re-register, including "the prescribed fee of $5.00," if the group intended to solicit in the state.[4]

More than two years later, New York authorities wrote to Mr. Nader personally and requested that he submit the center's annual reports for 1972 to 1974. In pertinent part, the Bureau's January 5, 1976, letter reads:

> Our office receives several requests each year for copies of this organization's annual report. Unfortunately, in each case, we must tell the party making the request that the organization's registration is cancelled. In view of the type of work this organization is committed to, it does not seem proper that it should fail in its responsibility to file annual reports with this office.[5]

In the same letter, the Bureau also requested Mr. Nader to identify any other organization associated with him which solicits contributions from the public in New York:

> The principal provision for filing such annual reports is to have a public record available of the financial activities of organizations which solicit contributions from the public.
>
> In this connection, we would ask you to advise if there are other organizations associated

with you who are soliciting contributions in New York State. If so, I would appreciate their names and addresses in order for us to determine whether their registration is required.[6]

The Bureau requested a reply within 20 days.

On January 9, 1976, CSRL's accountant Harvey Jester responded that "The Center has not raised funds in New York State since 1971, does not presently solicit funds there, nor does it have such plans for the future."[7] Mr. Jester added, "I think it would be useful for you to inform those who make inquiries that the Center is not required to furnish registration statements to your office."[8]

Mr. Jester's letter did not respond to that portion of the Bureau's request relating to any other organizations associated with Mr. Nader which solicit contributions in New York. The Bureau reiterated its request with greater specificity: "Please advise the relationship of your organization to Public Citizen, Inc. We recently have received many inquiries concerning this organization."[9]

Public Citizen eventually registered with the Bureau in May 1976, despite having placed a full-page advertisement soliciting contributions in the New York Times more than four years earlier.[10]

Capital Legal Foundation found additional instances of the Nader network's reluctance to respond to reasonable inquiries. For example, in response to inquiries received from the public, the Council of Better Business Bureaus (BBB) unsuccessfully attempted to gather information about Public Citizen in 1977 and 1978. The Council's Philanthropic Advisory Service (PAS), which conducted the research, informed the Capital Legal Foundation:

We [PAS] hand-delivered a questionnaire to Public Citizen on November 17, 1977, and sent two certified questionnaires on January 31, 1978, and March 1, 1978. Because we received no response to these requests for information, we prepared the July 1978 report which states "PAS has repeatedly requested but has not received current information about governance, programs and finances." In addition, we sent a copy of the report to the organization on July 10, 1978, along with another questionnaire. The group did not respond to this letter either. A copy of the questionnaire which was sent to the group is enclosed for your reference.[11]

The PAS report on Public Citizen concludes with the comment:

Because Public Citizen is not a charity, the BBB Standards for Charitable Solicitations do not apply. PAS believes, however, that any organization soliciting the general public for support should disclose on request information that potential donors may reasonably wish to consider.[12]

On April 9, 1980, Mr. Nader was asked, during the question and answer period following a public speech at George Washington University, why Public Citizen did not respond to the Better Business Bureau's information requests. Mr. Nader said that Public Citizen didn't respond "because they [BBB] are pro-business and would not give us a fair shake."[13]

The National Information Bureau also unsuccessfully attempted to gather information about Public Citizen. The NIB is a nonprofit organization whose purposes are "(1) to maintain sound standards in its field of philanthropy and (2) to help thoughtful contributors to give wisely." In a report released on October 1, 1979, the NIB stated:

NIB wrote to Public Citizen several times since 1971, most recently on September 5, 1978, and July 19, 1979, requesting up-to-date information generally made readily available to sound philanthropic organizations. . . . As of the date of this report, the requested information had not been supplied to us.[14]

The experience of U.S. Representative Thomas Kindness (R-OH) also illustrates these difficulties. In 1979, two employees of Mr. Nader's Public Citizen testified before a House of Representatives subcommittee in *opposition* to a proposed lobbying disclosure bill (H.R. 81, 96th Congress). The bill would have provided citizens with a better understanding of the legislative process and the identity of organizations trying to influence that process. During the course of the testimony, Representative Kindness asked Alan Morrison[15] and Andrew Feinstein[16] of Public Citizen where Mr. Nader maintains his offices.

Representative Kindness never received a definite answer:

Mr. Kindness.	Where is that [Mr. Nader's] office?
Mr. Morrison.	I'm sorry, where is it?
Mr. Kindness.	You say he has an office.
Mr. Morrison.	Yes, he has several places.
Mr. Kindness.	It's funny we never [have] been able to find out where.

Mr. Morrison.	You can find him if you want to get in touch with him, there is no problem.
Mr. Kindness.	I would be happy to be given some guidance in that respect as to where his office is.
Mr. Morrison.	Do you want to know a place where if you wanted to write him a letter you could reach him or you want the telephone number or what is it?
Mr. Kindness.	I see that I am not going to get the answer voluntarily.[17]

Capital Legal Foundation also experienced difficulty obtaining information from network organizations. For example, when Capital first attempted to contact the Center for the Study of Responsive Law, it was discovered the Center does not list its telephone number in the Washington, D.C., telephone directory even though the group maintains its headquarters in the District. Once the phone number was obtained, we called and spoke to a CSRL staff researcher and writer, Ronald Brownstein. We asked him for any general information he might provide about the Nader network. Mr. Brownstein's response was a series of questions concerning the nature of The Capital Legal Foundation. We answered all of them. (It is our policy to answer all questions.)

Mr. Brownstein said he would return our call "in a day or two."[18] After waiting a week, we phoned Mr. Brownstein again. He refused to tell us anything without first clearing it through Mr. Nader, and again stated that he would call us "in a few days."[19]

Another week passed and we did not receive a response from Mr. Brownstein. We decided to pursue another lead. The author of a recent newspaper article on Ralph Nader[20] told us that an assistant to Mr. Nader at the Center for The Study of Responsive Law, Kerry Barnett, had been most helpful in providing information and arranging an interview with Mr. Nader.

Accordingly, we telephoned Mr. Barnett. Although Mr. Barnett did not actually give us any information at that time, he said he would mail us a packet of brochures and invited us to call him again if we had any questions after reading them.[21] Mr. Barnett also referred us to Mike Horrocks, director of Public Citizen's Visitors Center, for general information about the Nader organizations.[22]

We immediately phoned Mr. Horrocks, but he was unavailable. After waiting more than five hours for a call which we were told would be promptly returned, we called him again. During the ensuing conversation, Mr. Horrocks referred us to Emmy Smith, an accountant for several Nader organizations. Mr. Horrocks informed us that he was acting pursuant to Mr. Nader's personal instructions.[23]

According to Mr. Horrocks, Mr. Barnett had personally consulted with Mr. Nader after our previous conversation with Mr. Barnett.[24] At this point, Mr. Nader reportedly issued an order that we should only be allowed to speak with Ms. Smith.

When we phoned Ms. Smith, she said she didn't have time to talk to us. As a result of our entreaties, she informed us that Mr. Nader is only affiliated with "Public Citizen, the Center for Study of Responsive Law, and a few other organizations."[25] Ms. Smith then reiterated that she absolutely had no more time, and terminated the conversation.

We called her the following day. She accepted the call and stated: "You should just stick to your business and let us do ours."[26] Again, we were only able to obtain information of the most general sort before Ms. Smith reminded us that she had no time to speak with us. We asked why Mr. Nader directed us to her if she could not be of assistance to us. "He and I are the two people who have to do with more than one group," Ms. Smith explained.[27]

Later that day we called Messrs. Brownstein and Barnett. Mr. Brownstein referred us back to Ms. Smith, whom he had not mentioned during our prior conversation with him.[28] Mr. Barnett also directed us to Ms. Smith, whom he said was the only person who could tell us what we need to know about the Nader organizations.[29] When we reminded him that (1) he had previously urged us to contact him if we needed further assistance, and (2) he had not mentioned Ms. Smith during the prior conversation, he simply reiterated that she was the one to whom we must speak.

Mr. Horrocks, director of the Visitors Center, eventually agreed to grant us an interview in his public relations capacity. The interview was conducted on June 5, 1980, at the Visitors Center. He provided us with general information on Public Citizen and its subdivisions but it was merely a regurgitation of information contained in the brochures distributed at the Visitors Center. Mr. Horrocks voluntarily stated that Mr. Nader is associated with Public Citizen, its subdivisions, and CSRL. Upon further inquiry, he mentioned two other groups that are associated with Mr. Nader: The Corporate Accountability Research Group and the Public Interest Research Group.

Mr. Horrocks stated that he had never heard of the Safety Systems Foundation, to which Mr. Nader was the sole contributor, at least until the end of 1979, or the Public Safety Research Institute, of which Mr. Nader is president and treasurer.

After our interview with Mr. Horrocks, we tried to schedule an interview with Mr. Nader through Mr. Barnett, but he did not return repeated phone calls.[30] We followed up by sending written requests via certified mail to both Mr. Barnett and Mr. Nader. Both refused to accept the letters and they were returned to us, *unopened.*

In early July we managed to contact Mr. Barnett at his office. He informed us that Mr. Nader was unavailable for interviews until mid-August. Mr. Barnett stated that he could not schedule an appointment with Mr. Nader at that time because it was too far in the future.[31]

By and large our efforts to obtain information from Nader groups were not successful. Three representatives of CSRL refused to provide us with specific information.[32] Spokespersons for two Nader groups never returned our calls, and when we called it was difficult to get through to them.[33] One group promised us information but never provided it.[34] Spokespersons of ten groups spoke with us briefly and only provided sketchy information.[35]

CONCLUSIONS

In our opinion, the events leading to the cancellation of the Center for the Study of Responsive Law's registration by New York State authorities are particularly telling. They demonstrate clearly CSRL's callous and contemptuous disregard for state disclosure laws aimed at protecting the public from fraudulent solicitation. The Center, it should be remembered, is supposedly representative of the public interest. We believe, however, that CSRL's actions in New York constitute a flagrant example of a mean-spirited refusal to give the public basic information about the organization's programs, governance and finances.

Similarly, Public Citizen's delay in registering is equally deplorable. The delay is inexcusable because Nader representatives knew or should have known that registration by Public Citizen was required when the Bureau investigated the Center in 1972.

Alan Morrison's refusal to disclose Nader's office address to Representative Kindness in 1979 also warrants criticism. Morrison's reluctance to provide a member of Congress with seemingly innocuous information is reprehensible in itself. When combined with opposition to a bill (H.R. 81, 96th Congress) designed to inform the public about involvement of special-interest groups in the legislative process, such conduct is even more deplorable. This particular lobbying disclosure bill was designed to serve the public interest by requiring disclosure from all who engage in such activity. Opposition to the bill by a group that portrays itself as an advocate of equal access to information is hypocritical.

The Capital Legal Foundation limited the subject matter of its interviews of network organizations to information one might reasonably expect a public interest group to disclose. We confined our inquiries to matters pertaining to: (1) tax and legal status; (2) organizational purposes and activities; (3) organizational governance; and (4) public filings under the Internal Revenue Code and relevant state or federal statutes. Capital did not solicit information pertaining to confidential matters such as the identity of contributors or minutes of board meetings. To the extent that research produced information on the finances of network groups, it was obtained from public sources such as IRS Form 990s.

Surreptitious methods were not used during the course of Capital's inquiries. We obtained information in an honest and forthright manner. Capital's interviewers always indicated the nature of their organization and volunteered to answer all questions concerning the Foundation. Detailed notes were taken of all correspondence and communications with the network groups, and files were maintained meticulously to insure accuracy and fairness. (For more data on Capital's research techniques and interviews see appendices A and B.)

Despite the limited scope and forthright manner of Capital's inquiries, it encountered and documented a consistent pattern of evasion and uncooperativeness on the part of most Nader organizations. In view of these difficulties—as well as the aforementioned experiences of the Council of Better Business Bureaus, the National Information Bureau, and the New York State Bureau of Charitable and Proprietary Organizations—it is Capital's opinion that the Nader organizations do not feel any obligation to comply with the most basic standards of disclosure, accessibility, and organizational accountability.

The Nader network's uncooperative response to inquiries by Capital and others is particularly reprehensible and incongruous given Mr. Nader's own repeated demands for openness, accountability, and public disclosure with respect to government and business. Any publicly owned company in the U.S. that refused to give similar information to the Securities and Exchange Commission, its shareholders, or the public at large would probably find its executives in jail and its stock banned from trading. Such a company might also find itself being criticized by Mr. Nader or one of his network organizations.

Mr. Nader and his groups cannot have it both ways. On the one hand, they agitate for more and more corporate and governmental disclosure to the public. On the other, they do not feel a duty themselves to make such public disclosures. In our opinion, organizations that presume to speak in the name of the "public interest" have an incontrovertible obligation to make information about their operations openly accessible to that very same "public."

Surely no group, company, or government official has to hide under a shroud of secrecy, unless there is something to hide. Ralph Nader has voiced a similar opinion as well. "Information," he said, "is the currency of democracy. Its denial must always be suspect."[36] At the Capital Legal Foundation, we endorse wholeheartedly this view. But we wonder why Mr. Nader and his groups do not live by his own words.

NOTES

1. Letter dated September 21, 1972, from Robert Cozzens of the New York State Bureau of Charitable and Proprietary Organizations.

2. Ibid.

3. Letter dated April 25, 1973, from Bureau of Charitable and Proprietary Organizations, Charitable Registrations Section.

4. Letter dated October 16, 1973, from Mr. Friedman, Senior Accountant of Charities Registration for the Bureau of Charitable and Proprietary Organizations.

5. Letter dated January 5, 1976, from Joseph G. Shea, Associate Accountant for the Bureau of Charitable and Proprietary Organizations.

6. Ibid.

7. Letter dated January 9, 1976.

8. Ibid.

9. Letter dated February 27, 1976.

10. A full-page ad from Public Citizen, Inc., soliciting contributions appeared in the *New York Times* on October 31, 1971.

11. Letter dated June 18, 1980, from Liz Foster, Research Writer, Philanthropic Advisory Service.

12. Philanthropic Advisory Service (Council of Better Business Bureaus, Inc.) Report dated July 1978.

13. Ralph Nader. Speech at George Washington University, 4/9/81.

14. NIB Report #1927.

15. Morrison is the director of Public Citizen Litigation Group.

16. Feinstein was employed by Public Citizen's Congress Watch.

17. Testimony of Alan Morrison, during hearings on H.R. 81 before subcommittee of House of Representatives, 96th Congress, 1979.

18. Phone conversation with Mr. Brownstein on May 21, 1980.

19. Phone conversation with Mr. Brownstein on May 27, 1980.

20. Louise Sweeney, "Ralph Nader: America's Last Angry Man" in *Christian Science Monitor*, 4/29/81.

21. Phone conversation with Mr. Barnett on June 2, 1980.

22. Ibid.

23. Phone conversation with Mr. Horrocks on June 2, 1980.

24. Ibid.

25. Phone conversation with Ms. Smith on June 2, 1980.

26. Phone conversation with Ms. Smith on June 3, 1980.

27. Ibid.

28. Phone conversation with Mr. Brownstein on June 3, 1980.

29. Phone conversation with Mr. Barnett on June 3, 1980.

30. We phoned Mr. Barnett three times, on June 18, 19, and 20, 1980. None of these calls was returned.

31. Phone conversation with Mr. Barnett on July 8, 1980.

32. Ron Brownstein, CSRL, 5/21/80, 6/3/80; Kerry Barnett, CSRL, 6/3/80, 7/8/80; Emmy Smith, CSRL, 7/9/80.

33. Kerry Barnett, CSRL, 6/18/80, 6/19/80, 6/20/80; Ron Brownstein CSRL, 5/21/80, 5/27/80, 6/3/80—said he would call us back in a "couple of days," and never did. Emmy Smith, CSRL, 7/8/80, Samuel Wolfe, Health Research Group, 7/9/80.

34. Jennifer McKenna, Equal Justice Foundation.

35. Emmy Smith (6/2/80, 6/3/80); Kerry Barnett (7/8/80) of Center for Study of Responsive Law; Harvey Jester, 7/8/80 and 7/9/80, and

Safety Systems Foundation; Kathy Fiorello, Tax Reform Research Group, 7/9/80 (Asked us to send our questions in writing, and returned them with little or no comment.); Mike Horrocks, Public Citizens Visitors Center 6/5 interview; Rachel Shimshack, Congress Watch, 7/8/80; Marilyn Osterman, PIRG and Corporate Accountability Research Group on 7/8/80; Frank O'Brien, Public Citizen Support Office, 7/9/80; David Vladeck, Public Citizen Litigation Group, 7/8/80.

36. "Ralph Nader Reports," *Ladies Home Journal,* September 1973.

Chapter 8
Conclusions

Ralph Nader first came to the public's attention with the dawn of the "anti-establishment" era in the early 1960s. It was a time of trauma, foreboding, instability, and dramatically rapid change for the United States both at home and abroad.

The civil rights movement put America's morality and democratic values to a severe and sorely needed test. The "Cuban Missile Crisis" placed the nation on the precipice of nuclear war. The assassination of President John F. Kennedy sorrowfully revealed our vulnerability as a free country in a hostile world. The following year the electorate strongly rebuked Barry Goldwater's call for less governmental authority and more individual responsibility, and President Lyndon B. Johnson embarked on the "Great Society" programs of social welfare, which have endured for nearly 20 years.

In the early 1960s, it is now clear, Americans began to feel that the individual in society, without strong help from the government, could not cope with the enormity of modern-day problems. Government, therefore, assumed a greater role in American society than ever before. Other traditional institutions, such as the free-enterprise economic system, were increasingly distrusted.

This was also a tender and innocent age, a time of utopian dreams. The Cold War was ending. Pax Americana seemed a real possibility. Rapid technological change promised both economic prosperity and quick fixes to both old and new problems. Dreamers like Kennedy and King foretold a radiant future.

This time of instability and shift was opportune for Mr. Nader. In an earlier era, his criticism of the automobile, one of America's most common and cherished possessions, would have sparked widespread derision. He might even have been feared as a threat to traditional American values. But, with the emerging distrust of the "establishment" in the 1960s, Mr. Nader was embraced by many Americans, who viewed him as a modern-day David doing battle with the Goliath of industry. This is not to say that Mr. Nader was seen as a savior. There was no popular cry, say, for his election to public office or to take over the management of General Motors. Rather, he was a rallying point, a seemingly apolitical voice echoing the common man's frustrations.

Since those "anti-establishment" days, much has changed. For whatever reasons, corporations have become more sensitive and responsive to public pressure. For instance, car designers show a greater concern for safety. The federal government has vastly increased in size and in the scope of its activities, probably even beyond LBJ's dreams. There is very little, if any, talk of "opposition to the establishment." Instead, life in America has become so politicized that some would say—such as economist Milton Friedman in his book and television series, "Free to Choose"—that government has become too paternalistic and now denies the individual the freedom to choose.

In the meantime, "public interest" groups have developed as the offspring of what David Lebedoff calls "the new elite" in the socio-economic-political order. These advocacy organizations have worked to change the function of government and the operation of the economy. To a great extent, their efforts have been successful, as the increase in governmental regulation over the past decade testifies. Missing, however, has been a general recognition that the "public interest" movement has become de facto a new political entity or even a new party. These groups are not typically referred to as a political movement or party because of their use of the seemingly apolitical aegis of the "public interest." This shield tends to deflect any criticism, and even questioning, of their political and ideological motives. Furthermore, the "public interest" symbol imparts the oftentimes erroneous impression that these groups enjoy a large amount of broad public support.

Despite their "public interest" motto, however, most of these groups have a particular political ideology, a set agenda for economic, political and social change, and limited constituencies. They are, in fact, *special interest* groups and no different from any other group that attempts to lobby public opinion and garner governmental support for a particular cause. Their use of the "public interest" label is a ruse and a disguise.

This deception is aided by the mode of operation of these so-called "public interest" groups. They eschew declaring themselves as political parties, nominating candidates for public office, holding conventions of party members, writing party platforms, soliciting *taxable* contributions and, most important, opening themselves up to public scrutiny and criticism. To date, these groups have shown a distinct reluctance to operate in such an open and forthright manner.

Instead, they prefer certain backdoor methods of influencing the political and economic system. These groups sometimes lobby and often provide "research" data on special interest bills and regulations. They occasionally use the court system—often in the form of "class action" suits—to get government or corporations to agree to their demands for, say, more environmental regulation. Most of these groups did not try to develop a large membership, to which they would then have to be responsible, although they often solicit funds from the public. Rather they keep their ranks small in order to pursue any tangential cause they wish. Their organizational structure also tends to ward off much public scrutiny, as the Capital Legal Foundation found out quickly in its investigation of the organizations associated with Ralph Nader. They do not publish much about their political philosophies or agendas, and often what is published is too vague to be truly informative.

What is clear from their activities, however, is the belief that they distrust our present economic and political system. They doubt the efficacy of individual choice, preferring, instead, paternalism and collective decision-making. They do not seem to believe that in many cases American consumers are concerned or careful enough to pick the best and safest products at prices they are willing to pay. Instead, these groups advocate federal government regulations that will help make the consumer's choices for him. They do not trust the investor's discretion in selecting companies for investment. Rather these groups want more government regulations to ensure "corporate accountability," even to those who do not hold stock in, work for, or buy a company's products. More governmental intervention into the economy is seen as only beneficial, despite the historical examples in the United States and elsewhere to the contrary. There appears to be an underlying perception among these groups that individuals who want to make money and prosper are not to be trusted. Even public officials who support the free-enterprise system are suspect in the eyes of "public interest" advocates.

In place of our system of modified and limited individual choice and private enterprise — we certainly recognize and welcome much of what FDA, SEC, EPA and similar agencies do — the "public interest" groups would appear to want more politicalization of life in America. In other words, government would probably become more authoritarian or even totalitarian by encroaching more on our private lives as workers, employers, and consumers. And it has been and would be a government they run.

This is a distinct political ideology, which has been and remains in vogue in Western thought. But it is a radical departure from U.S. political tradition of the last 200 years, and it does not square with the common view of the nature of the public interest.

For these reasons it is important to know more about Ralph Nader's activities and the work of his associated groups. Mr. Nader personifies the "public interest" advocate par excellence. For many Americans, he still appears as a poor, selfless individual, speaking out on behalf of the "common man." What the Capital Legal Foundation's research has shown is that such an image is far from the truth.

A Nader network exists, although its existence has not previously been exposed to much public light. The network consists of at least 19 groups, including the subgroups of Public Citizen and the Center for the Study of Responsive Law. Indeed, the network may be even larger, but the difficulty the Foundation had in getting information from the groups kept the list to only

19. Such a number is still, of course, large, and their one common denominator is a discernible link with Ralph Nader.

Mr. Nader's relationship to the network groups, however, is often concealed from the public. Initially, spokespersons for these groups informed the Capital Legal Foundation that Mr. Nader was affiliated with only four organizations in the network. The existence of the remaining ties was learned through independent and, perforce, dogged investigation and research.

Although the organizations generally purport to be autonomous—and some in fact are relatively independent—they do have strong, discernible connections with Mr. Nader. To be sure, he does not control all of the network groups in a legal or managerial sense, but he does exert considerable influence over the various groups that he personally funds or indirectly funds via grants from the organizations that he formally controls.

We need state no view of the propriety of Mr. Nader's affiliation with so many groups. That he is involved with such a large number is a testament to his energy and even more to his ambition. The secrecy that shrouds these ties is disturbing, however. Why is Mr. Nader so reluctant to divulge his associations with these groups?

The inevitable answer is that Mr. Nader and his associates do not want the public to know the extent and reach of his power and influence. He therefore endeavors to hide this concentration of power by obfuscating the nature of his relationships to the organizations and by emphasizing their supposed autonomy. That he conceals the extent of his influence and power is not surprising. Mr. Nader and his network vehemently attack concentrations of power which they claim exist in other areas of our society.

It is our opinion that market segmentation is an additional motive behind Mr. Nader's veil of network secrecy. By creating an increasing number of apparently separate organizations, each with its own fund-raising efforts, Mr. Nader is able to attract a greater aggregate share of the public's charitable contributions.

Mr. Nader prefers to manipulate the press, public opinion, and government partly from behind the scenes rather than in the public eye, where he might be held accountable and subjected to public scrutiny. Moreover, a public aware of the scope of the Nader operations and power might be somewhat more skeptical of his scolding diatribes against other groups in our society. A skeptical public would demand the proof of the alleged harms that Mr. Nader often lacks.

The ability of one person to exercise, free of much public scrutiny, let alone control, so much power and influence over policies and programs of a multitude of organizations raises very serious concern. Foremost is the likelihood that these so-called "public interest" groups represent only one man's view of the "common good." In other words, that they assume the character of any other *special interest* lobby.

The Nader network resembles a huge lobbying and opinion-making conglomerate. . . It is characterized by interlocking directorates, transfers of funds among fellow organizations, a shared ideology, often shared personnel and facilities, and an abiding passion for secrecy. In many respects, the network resembles the "image" of corporations which Mr. Nader and his groups criticize.

Such contradictions and hypocrisy are a common characteristic of the Nader network, and nowhere is this more evident than with respect to public disclosure of information. On the one hand, the groups advocate open government and corporate disclosure of confidential data. Yet, as "public interest" organizations, they disavow any reciprocal obligation to subject their own processes to public scrutiny. Their organizational structure—for example, the Center for the Study of Responsive Law and Safety Systems are trusts—often helps to avoid such scrutiny by the general public. Few of the groups are membership organizations with the attendant obligation to make public reports and to allow members a voice in the running of the group.

This shroud of secrecy has even extended to requests from responsible public officials. At least two groups, Public Citizen and NCCB, have generally neglected to comply with state charitable solicitation laws, which are designed to ensure that charitable groups disclose pertinent information to the contributing public.

Network finances are not the only jealously guarded secrets: the network refuses to divulge the number of its full-time employees; some groups, such as CSRL, do not list their telephone numbers in the directory; office addresses are sometimes not divulged, as is the case with Public Citizen; reasonable public inquiries and requests for information are ignored; and many network officials and Mr. Nader himself are inaccessible to the public.

The secrecy of the network is indeed anomalous when one considers that the network vigorously supports the Freedom of Information Act, which requires the federal government to disclose information to the public, and has demanded greater corporate disclosure.

Yet, the apparent inconsistency is explainable if one accepts that the only thing consistent about the network's behavior is its hypocrisy—its devotion to one set of laws for "public interest" groups and another for everyone else.

As a case in point, contrast Public Citizen's strong support for the Freedom of Information Act with its simultaneous and equally vigorous opposition to a disclosure bill (H.R. 81, 96th Congress) designed to inform the public of the role special interest groups—such as the network lobbying arms—play in passage or defeat of legislation. If it is important to know what the government is doing that affects the public, why is it not important to know what "public interest" groups or other lobbyists are doing that affects the government and eventually the public?

"Information is the currency of democracy; its denial must always be suspect,"[1] Mr. Nader boldly asserts. Indeed, it is a statement that rings of immutable truth. For Mr. Nader, however, it appears to be little more than the articulation of a majestic platitude. His conduct in providing information to the public about the activities of his network of organizations leaves much to be desired, and admits of the conclusion that Mr. Nader is a better rhetorician than practitioner of public disclosure. Conduct rather than rhetoric is the proper measure of Mr. Nader's real contribution to the public interest, and in that regard, his reluctance to disclose information to the public is indeed suspect. Moreover, when this reluctance assumes the form of failure to comply with the law, it is more than suspect; it is insidious.

The Capital Legal Foundation found that at least two network groups, Public Citizen and National Citi-

zens Committee for Broadcasting, did not comply with
state charitable solicitation laws. Public Citizen is now
registered in some states, including New York, but this
occurred only after repeated prodding by New York
State officials. Nonetheless, there may be more infractions of charitable solicitation laws in many states by
other network organizations. It is a question that has
received scant attention from most governmental authorities and deserves more investigation.

The known infractions of law, however, are
plain. They are deplorable especially for organizations
that claim to serve the "public interest." The explicit
purpose of these statutes is to promote public disclosure
and to protect the public from fraud. The public interest
is not well-served when self-proclaimed protectors of
the "public interest" demonstrate such flagrant disregard for the letter and the spirit of the law. This conduct
is particularly egregious and reprehensible when one
considers that some network groups vehemently castigate corporations for allegedly flouting the law. Apparently, these groups subscribe to the view: "Do as we
say, and not as we do."

A society based on a regime of law cannot toler-
ate double standards. Otherwise, the law will soon become debased and worthless. Moreover, groups that
self-righteously portray themselves as the last bastion of
the "public interest" have an absolute duty to abide by
the law as determined through the democratic process.
That some groups do not acknowledge these reciprocal
duties shows an intolerable contempt for the law and
the public.

The refusals of Public Citizen and NCCB to comply with state solicitation statutes are but two examples
of the unwillingness of some network groups to account
for funds obtained from the public. Other examples are

the speculative stock market transactions of Public Safety Research Institute and Safety Systems Foundation. Some of their transactions raise serious ethical and policy questions. For example, the use of tax-exempt charitable dollars to engage in stock speculation violates the spirit, if not the letter, of the law. The Internal Revenue Service apparently also holds this view and has investigated several Nader "charities." Some of these have settled with the IRS and paid relatively substantial amounts to the IRS.

At a less legalistic level, there is something suspect about using these monies for such purposes without disclosing these investments in annual reports to contributors. Contributors, while they cannot dictate how their money is used, are at least entitled to fair disclosure.

Little recognized is the fact that federal tax regulations for charitable groups have helped Mr. Nader's organizations amass a not-so-small fortune. The premise underlying these tax-exemption rules is that charities "give more than they get" and such service to humanity should not be inhibited by the government's need for revenue. The tax laws even include a positive inducement for contributing to charities—that is, taxpayers are allowed to deduct these donations when figuring out their taxes.

In the case of the Nader network organizations, these tax-exemption principles have been turned on their head. By spending far less money than they get, these groups may have filled their coffers beyond the limits of what the public might have expected from advocacy organizations. The Capital Legal Foundation's research of only 6 of the 19 Nader network organizations revealed a net worth of $3.4 million at the end of 1978, the latest year of complete financial data, and the sum may well have grown since then. It is, of course, understandable for organizations that are dependent on public support to store away a nest egg to alleviate the vicissitudes of private donation trends. But the financial decisions of these six Nader groups appear to go far beyond the bounds of normal fiscal conservatism.

There is little evidence that these network groups have used their funds to pursue their stated charitable purposes. In some cases, these funds have been used in questionable stock market transactions. In other instances, the money has been used to help finance another sister group in the network. The Tax Reform Act of 1969 tried to prevent abuses of charitable contributions by requiring minimum distribution rules. These regulations, however, have done little to impede the self-aggrandizement of the Nader network.

Indeed, the network formation facilitates fundraising and the transfer of money among network groups. The "public interest" label provides an illusion of broad public support and entices donations from individuals who otherwise would probably not contribute to special interest causes. In addition, the stratification of the network makes it appear smaller and more needy than it actually is. Who among Mr. Nader's supporters or critics knows that the network possesses millions of dollars?

The network format also obfuscates the distinction between the groups' research and political lobbying activities. This distinction is particularly important in light of Internal Revenue Service rules on tax-exempt status. Tax-exempt organizations are permitted to engage in a limited amount of political lobbying—for example, urging passage of a piece of legislation in Congress. If an organization pursues lobbying activities beyond those limits, its tax-exempt status can be revoked. In the case of the Nader network, some groups are ostensibly research outfits and others are more heavily engaged in lobbying activities. This distinction may be very clear on paper. But there is nothing in the IRS rules to stop someone from, say, walking down the hall from a tax-exempt research bureau and handing over a study or report to a lobbyist.

Despite this questionable overlap of research work and lobbying, the fact remains that the network engages in more lobbying than is generally recognized. Public Citizen, including its subgroups, retains at least 13 registered lobbyists, who often appear before Congress. Under Internal Revenue Code Section 501 (c) (4), Public Citizen is permitted to lobby, but contributors to the group cannot deduct their donations for tax purposes. Several other groups advocate before regulatory agencies. At least one network group, Aviation Consumer Action Project, has engaged in lobbying in the past, in spite of the IRS restrictions imposed by Section 501 (c) (3).[2]

For obvious tax considerations, many network groups disavow that they engage in lobbying. Technically, their disavowals are probably accurate. But they do not ring true if one considers the symbiotic relationship between the research and lobbying arms of the network. The research groups are think-tanks for the lobbying groups. Research is not undertaken for academic or descriptive purposes. Usually it is undertaken with a specific political lobbying objective in mind, and then the research is handed over to the lobbyists. Such activities raise serious questions of whether some Nader network groups are abusing their tax-exempt status. It is a determination that only the IRS can make, and so far it has shown only a limited interest.

The network's range of issues is much more delimited than its "public interest" label would lead one to believe. The highest priority is given to more governmental regulation of corporations, "open" government, occupational health and safety, "consumer activism" and, of course, self-preservation of the Nader network. The common thread that runs throughout most of these issues is the advocacy for more governmental regulation.

Several network groups are exclusively devoted to promoting more governmental regulation of businesses. These groups apparently believe that governmental intervention is the solution to most social and economic ills. However, these "public interest" groups pay little, if any, attention to the economic cost of regulation. Not only do these regulations increase the size and cost of government and the expense of running a company, but scarce money and manpower is diverted to fulfilling the demands of federal bureaucrats and "public interest" advocates. To that extent, there are less resources available for investment in new plant and equipment. Fewer new jobs are created, and the growth of new goods and services is retarded. In other words, the indiscriminate increase in federal regulations has an adverse impact on the average standard of living in the United States.

This impact falls disproportionately on the poor, who benefit most from the marginal increases in economic growth. The creation of new jobs, the expansion of educational and career opportunities, the decline in the relative prices of goods and services, and the ability of government to fund social welfare programs all depend on gains in economic productivity. Governmental regulation of the economy saps the potential for increased productivity, and makes everyone worse off, especially the poor.

Mr. Nader's "public interest" groups pay little heed to such matters. Indeed, these groups are relatively indifferent to the concerns of the poor, minorities, and the working class in our society. Moreover, these so-called "public interest" regulations stymie the growth of the economy and, as a result, constrict the opportunities and benefits for the poor. How many of America's poor would be better off today if not for the slow pace of economic growth due to excessive federal regulation? This question apparently never dawns on Mr. Nader's "public interest" advocates when they lobby in Washington for more governmental regulation of the economy.

This failure to appreciate the broader consequences of "public interest" advocacy probably has much to do with Mr. Nader's own idiosyncracies. Many issues seized upon by the network organizations merely reflect Mr. Nader's personal experience or biases. For example, the impetus for organizing the Aviation Consumer Action Project came from the time he was bumped off a commercial airline flight. Similarly, Mr. Nader, who was once an avid hitchhiker, personally attributes his concern over automobile safety to his travel experiences, when he noticed the sometimes gruesome results of auto collisions.[3]

The inherent danger in coupling one's own feelings and political views with the "public interest" label is simply that you will get it wrong. On occasion, an individual's opinion may coincide with the "public interest." But such a coincidence is infrequent by the very nature of the fact that the "public interest" is achieved through the formulation of a consensus among competing and conflicting views. The "public interest" is everyone's view and, at the same time, no one's view.

Mr. Nader's preoccupation with his own interests and his use of the "public interest" motto can sometimes produce absurd exaggerations. In regard to nuclear energy, for instance, Mr. Nader said: "If they don't close these reactors down, we'll have civil war in five years."[4] His statement was certainly not reflective of general public opinion. It did not make a positive contribution to the debate about the usefulness or possible dangers of nuclear power plants. Rather, it introduced a degree of hysteria that could not possibly serve the true public interest.

Such debasement of public debate is not an uncommon practice for Mr. Nader. In a 1979 interview, he seemed to eschew ad hominem attacks against his critics and preferred to argue the merits of an issue. "I focus on the issues," he said. "I don't personalize people. I mean, GM [General Motors] is bad because GM is bad. I don't go looking for personal failings like they did, you know."[5] (Mr. Nader's reference to GM obviously deals with its admission of investigating his background after the publication of his book on automobile safety, *Unsafe at Any Speed*. Mr. Nader brought a lawsuit against the company, and GM eventually paid him $425,000 in an out-of-court settlement.)

In spite of this apparent rejection of ad hominem mud-slinging, Mr. Nader has in several instances demeaned the debate on important national policy issues by engaging in hysterical verbal attacks on his opponents. It was reported in the press that during consideration of the Consumer Protection Act in 1977, which Mr. Nader ardently supported, he called one Congressman a "disgustingly repulsive, slimy double-crosser."[6] The bill was later defeated, and a number of Congressmen attributed the defeat to Mr. Nader's name-calling tactics.

In March 1979, the Gannett News Service reported that Mr. Nader called a Congressman, who opposed legislation on federally mandated automobile "air bags," a "pathological liar" and a "corrupt, lying, anti-people crook."[7] Mr. Nader also said that opponents of the "air bag" safety device were typical of someone who would "sell thalidomide [which has caused birth defects] to pregnant women."[8] These are some of the examples of Mr. Nader's contribution to debate in the name of the "public interest."

Nader's opposition to disclosure of network activities and finances further demonstrates his hypocrisy. Mr. Nader seeks to place all governmental and corporate activities in a fish bowl. On the other hand, Mr. Nader shrouds the allegedly "public interest" activities of his network, its structure and finances, in a veil of secrecy. Mr. Nader apparently does not agree with the old adage that "What's good for the goose is good for the gander."

A similar kind of hypocrisy can be found in the practices of some Nader network organizations, which are blatantly guilty of using the very same tactics that they condemn in others. Take the "negative check-off" system used on many college campuses to fund Public Interest Research Groups. According to author David Sanford, PIRGs have collected more than $1 million from students annually by using the "negative check-off" system.[9]

The system works similarly to some book and record clubs, which Mr. Nader's groups have criticized. Money is automatically taken out of every student's campus association fees and handed over to the local

PIRG at the start of each semester. The system is called "voluntary" because the student body must vote to accept the procedure and students who do not wish to financially support the PIRG can ask for their money back. The "voluntary contribution" claim, however, is far from the truth. The yearly turnover of the student bodies means that a PIRG contribution scheme approved years earlier can be imposed on students who never had a vote on the matter. Moreover, the PIRG fees, along with other charges, *must* be paid *before* the start of each semester in order to assure enrollment. Only after the initial payment is made can a student ask for his or her money back. Relatively few demand their money back, however.

The relatively small PIRG fee is obscured by the overwhelming tuition bill that normally runs into thousands of dollars. Moreover, college students are inundated with heaps of paperwork at the start of every semester, ranging from classroom assignments and administrative forms to writing letters back home. To "voluntarily" ask for another form to retrieve a few dollars from a PIRG is too much to expect of most college students. The financial success of these campus-based PIRGs is, therefore, more due to student apathy or distraction than passionate support of the "public interest" cause.

A few students, however, so objected to the "negative check-off" system that they asked for more than just their money back. Three Rutgers University students sued the New Jersey PIRG in U.S. District Court. The students alleged that the fee collection procedure unconstitutionally forced students to join organizations, albeit temporarily, that they would otherwise not join. In addition, these students alleged that the mandatory assessment and transmission of fees collected by Rutgers University, a state college, to finance a private lobbying group is yet another violation of the law. At the date of this writing, the district court's decision in favor of the university is on appeal.

Although the grass-roots challenge presented by the three Rutgers students is new to the "public interest" movement, the courtroom is not unfamiliar turf. Indeed, many "public interest" groups have discovered that litigation in the courts is a convenient means of changing public policy. Once a court decision is made, especially after an appeal, compliance is relatively quick and fairly uniform. Judicial rulings tend to accomplish results immediately, unlike attempts to sway opinion in the White House, on Capitol Hill, or among the public. It took "public interest" groups several years, however, to appreciate the potential opportunities afforded by the judicial process.

In their formative years, the Nader network organizations were generally research-oriented. The emphasis was on documenting problems, rather than formulating and implementing solutions. During the intermediate stage of the network's development, lobbying was the preeminent tactic.

In recent years, the emphasis on research has diminished, except insofar as it relates to lobbying. But even lobbying has assumed a less important role for "public interest" groups. The prevailing strategy is to affect change through litigation in the courts. Implicit in this shift is the recognition that the "consumer" movement is "seriously stalled,"[10] and new methods of attracting public attention and influencing public policy decisions needed to be found.

Besides the legal battling, the Nader network also managed to influence public policy with the appointment of at least two key officials in President Jimmy

Carter's administration. Joan T. Claybrook, former director of Mr. Nader's Congress Watch, became head of the National Highway Traffic Safety Administration, which directly sets standards for automotive safety and gas mileage. Reuben Robertson, a close Nader associate and employee from 1971 to 1978, became chairman of the Administrative Conference of the United States in July 1980, over the objections raised by several members of Congress and the Capital Legal Foundation. Indeed, Mr. Robertson's impact on public policy might have been immense if not for the defeat in Congress of a $20 million bill to provide "public interest" groups with funding to "intervene" in the federal decision-making process.

Apart from these political appointments, the Carter administration was well-disposed to the "public interest" cause. During the Carter years, almost every regulatory and legislative avenue lay supinely open to the "public interest" movement. Given such an opportunity, it is surprising that these "public interest" groups did not accomplish even more than they did. The Reagan administration is unlikely to give these groups much opportunity to restore their image.

This realization, in combination with declining public support, has led to the formation of the Alliance for Justice, a coalition of at least 17 "public interest," "consumer advocacy," and civil rights groups. Included among the Alliance organizations are the National Organization of Women, Natural Resources Defense Council, Consumers Union and the Center for Law in the Public Interest.[11] The Alliance replaced the Council for Public Interest Law.

Many "public interest" groups are in dire financial straits because foundation grants are drying up and public support is diminishing. The Alliance represents an effort to pool resources to develop a strategy that will ensure their survival. The central tactic of the new strategy is to get the federal government to supplement the revenue of these groups by paying their legal fees.[12]

Such a strategy is made possible by the practice developed in the arena of environmental litigation of intervenor funding for the purpose of allowing "public interest" groups to participate in proceedings before federal agencies. Furthermore, in 1980 the Congress passed the Equal Access to Justice Act, which provides that parties who prevail in adversary proceedings against the government are generally entitled to recover attorney fees, within prescribed parameters.

These federal programs raise the specter of lawsuits and proceedings being brought against the federal government not so much to defend or promote a principle but instead in hopes of winning some sort of recovery in order to perpetuate these "public interest" organizations. Successful implementation of the Alliance's strategy would mean that the American taxpayer would become a primary contributor to the coffers of these groups.

In reviewing all of these "public interest" groups' activities, an overriding question remains: Has the Nader network abused the public's trust?

When analyzing organizations that purport to represent the "public interest" and depend in part on public contributions, it is essential to consider the great amount of public trust placed in these groups. Any individual who donates his or her hard-earned money to a "public interest" group can legitimately expect that it will act in accordance with the philosophy used to attract the contributions in the first place. Any significant deviation from the organization's espoused philosophy constitutes a serious breach of trust.

151

In the case of "public interest" groups, the quintessence of their philosophy requires the openness and accountability of such public institutions as government and publicly held corporations. That these standards of conduct should also be adhered to religiously by any legitimate "public interest" organization is self-evident.

However, as Capital Legal Foundation's study revealed, several of the Nader organizations have failed to abide by these minimum standards of acceptable conduct. The same can be said of Ralph Nader, who occupies a unique position in the "public interest" movement. He is, or at least was, seen by the public as the embodiment of *the* "public interest" advocate, and as a result, contributors often made their donations not so much to his organizations but to the man. This status places Mr. Nader in a quasi-fiduciary relationship with respect to funds he and his groups receive and thus requires him to act according to the strictest code of public conduct.

Yet Capital Legal Foundation found that this has often not been the case. For instance, Mr. Nader's private foundations, which he funds with money from his personal income, invest heavily in utilities that generate electricity from nuclear power. But Mr. Nader publicly opposes nuclear power, as does Critical Mass Energy Project, which is a subgroup of Public Citizen. These same Nader foundations have invested in several other industries and corporations that he has publicly criticized. Needless to say, these investments are not generally made known to the public.

Moreover, the Nader network espouses only a vague notion of the "public interest." The issue-orientation of these groups, in practice, is very limited. Many are strictly single-issue organizations, and, viewed collectively, respond to a narrow range of issues.

Mr. Nader's view of the "public interest" is similarly vague, but perhaps deliberately so. By design, he retains direct control of the organizations with the broadest issue orientation. The other single-issue groups are "spun off" or relegated to secondary status as soon as they are adequately organized. That is, Mr. Nader typically disassociates himself from single-issue groups that he helps organize and/or funds.

This technique appears to be part and parcel of his strategy to avoid delimiting, in practice or definition, his "public interest" work. The effective result is that Mr. Nader is associated with vaguely defined general causes rather than specific issues. By picking and choosing among the general issues, Mr. Nader is free to decide at a given moment what is and what is not in the "public interest," and to do so on an *ad hoc* basis.

Correspondingly, since the boundaries of Nader's activities are in theory virtually unlimited, he is able to depict his work as an all-encompassing defense of the interests of the American public. So long as the scope of Nader's interests remains unspecified, it is difficult to assess his claim that he represents "the public interest." On the other hand, if Nader were linked only to specific issues or interests, as are the majority of network organizations, the apparent breadth of the public he purports to represent would narrow considerably. However, by aligning himself with organizations with an all-encompassing issue-orientation, Nader is able to decide, case by case, what lies in the public interest without ever having to precisely define or justify his concept of the public interest.

We do know something about what Nader

loathes—corporations and all connected with them. We do know what he is indifferent to—the concerns of the poor and the Black and the worker. But what does Mr. Nader stand for? What does he believe the "public interest" is? And who is the "public" he claims to represent?

Mr. Nader presupposes that a general consensus exists as to what constitutes the "public interest," but he conspicuously refuses to define it. The ultimate consequence is that Mr. Nader's interpretation of the "public interest" is made less vulnerable to public scrutiny. A biographer of Mr. Nader, Charles McCarry, expresses this point, but in less critical terms: "Nader is not called upon for explanations because it is accepted that he represents the public interest."[13] It is time that Mr. Nader be held accountable for his views and activities.

Mr. Nader and his organizations have accomplished many results that most citizens would regard as good and just; for example, food, drug, and pesticide labeling requirements. By helping to focus and mobilize broad public scrutiny into the processes of and influences upon government, Mr. Nader has served what we also believe to be a vital public interest objective. But there is one lesson history has painfully taught: that ends, however "good," do not justify the means.

This book is a critique of the means and tactics utilized by the Nader network. We have pointed to several areas—structure, finances, ideological bias, compliance with laws and regulations, and questionable tactics—where we believe the network's conduct has fallen far short of the standards of conduct demanded by the "public interest" label. Members of a free and democratic society must constantly scrutinize all those who purport to represent and defend the "public interest," and must demand a regular accounting. Left unchecked, groups like the Nader network, which seek to influence and manipulate governmental choices on behalf of narrowly defined special interests, could lead this country down the road toward tyranny and authoritarian government. This must not happen. The arbitration of what is in the public interest depends on a process that is free and open. We hope this book will contribute to the ongoing dialog about this process.

NOTES

1. "Ralph Nader Reports," *Ladies Home Journal,* September 1973.

2. 1978 Lobbying Registration Form filed with the Clerk of the House.

3. Charles McCarry, *Citizen Nader* (New York, Saturday Review Press), 1972, p. 56.

4. "Geiger Counter," *Voice,* April 4, 1977.

5. Barbara O'Reilley, "Nader Series," written for Gannett News Service, 3/29/79.

6. Ibid.

7. Ibid.; Julia Rose, "Ralph Nader Launches Anti-Shuster Campaign," written for States News Service, 6/23/78.

8. Barbara O'Reilley, "Nader Series."

9. David Sanford, *Me and Ralph* (Washington, D.C., New Republic Book Co.), 1976.

10. Joseph Lelyveld, "Nader Undaunted by Setbacks to Consumer Drive," *New York Times,* 11/24/81, p. 55.

11. Only Consumers Union and Center for Law in the Public Interest have or had any affiliation with Ralph Nader.

12. "Ambulance Chasers," *Wall Street Journal,* 2/26/81.

13. McCarry, *Citizen Nader,* p. 319.

Appendix A
Research Techniques

The Nader organizations were less than forthcoming in response to the requests for information by the Capital Legal Foundation. We therefore think it would be of value to the readers of this report to summarize our sources of information and the manner in which we conducted our research on the Nader network.

We limited our research to information one might reasonably expect a public interest organization to disclose—that is, tax and legal status, organizational purposes and projects, officers, and so forth. We scrupulously avoided inquiring into sensitive matters such as identities of contributors or minutes of board meetings.

In conducting our research and analyzing the information we obtained, we endeavored to remain objective and fair. To the extent practicable, we obtained information from neutral sources. However, much of the available information on the Nader network is neither objective nor neutral. Therefore, the report includes materials presenting both favorable and unfavorable perspectives.

The information contained in this report was obtained in an honest and forthright manner. We never used surreptitious methods to obtain information. The persons from whom we solicited information were always informed of (1) the name and interests of the organization we represent, and (2) the purpose of the study. We voluntarily answered any questions concerning the Capital Legal Foundation's operations and activities. When requested, we submitted our questions in written form and/or provided copies of our tax returns.

To insure accuracy and fairness, detailed notes were taken during telephone inquiries and personal interviews. We maintained meticulous records of all correspondence respecting information requests.

Information was obtained from various sources, including:

1. media accounts, expecially with respect to defunct organizations;

2. telephone interviews;

3. local government agencies with whom many organizations are required to register;

4. brochures and pamphlets published by the organizations;

5. federal agencies such as the Internal Revenue Service, with whom tax-exempt organizations are required to file a Form 990;

6. published literary works;

7. files maintained by foundations and organizations;

8. the articles of incorporation and by-laws of various Nader organizations;

9. transcripts of Senate and House of Representatives hearings;

10. the Library of Congress;

11. the Office of the Clerk of the House of Representatives; and

12. Freedom of Information Act requests.

The above delineation of sources of information is not exhaustive. A complete listing is contained in Appendix B.

The enumerated sources were more or less fruitful. Journalistic accounts had limited utility because they frequently contained unverifiable data. Telephone interviews were generally unproductive because several organizational representatives were not very responsive to our inquiries. This reluctance to cooperate is set forth with greater particularity in Chapter 7.

Information obtained from the IRS did not meet our expectations. Many of the requested documents were unavailable or outdated.

We initially believed that state charitable solicitation statutes would provide a fertile source of information, since organizations which publicly solicit contributions are required to register as charitable organizations and file annual reports. This source was not very productive because the Nader organizations we examined generally have not registered as charitable organizations. See Chapter 6 of this report.

The District of Columbia Corporate Records Office was a fertile source of information with respect to organizations incorporated in the District. This office provided us with copies of the articles of incorporation and by-laws of network organizations that had filed the requisite documents. The documents were useful in identifying members of the board of directors, the purpose(s) of the organization, and the identity of the incorporators. The aforementioned documents also disclosed interconnections between organizations of which we previously had been unaware. These interconnections are discussed in detail in Chapter 3, "Links Between Nader and Network Groups."

Transcripts of Senate and House hearings were also useful. Testimony by Mr. Nader and close associates was instrumental in identifying positions taken on various issues affecting the public interest, and the general policy orientation of the Nader network.

Records in the Office of the Clerk of the House of Representatives disclosed which Nader organizations were registered as lobbyists on Capitol Hill. The registration statements provided information on the issues the respective organizations were lobbying for or against.

Appendix B
Sources of Information

The sources of information, including telephone contacts, used to prepare this report were as follows (unless otherwise indicated, dates given are for 1980):

Alcey, Denise—Co-Ed., *Encyclopedia of Associations,* 313/961-2242, 5/30, 1:10.
Andrews, Douglas—Ohio Charitable Foundations Sections, 6/4, 11:00 a.m.
Arisumi, Steven—Exec. Dir., Md. PIRG, 301/454-5601, 8/15, 3:10.
Aron, Nan—Exec. Dir., Council on Public Interest Law, 202/624-8390, 5/20, p.m.
Baker, Mrs.—Md. Charitable Organizations Office, 301/269-3421, 6/4, 9:55 a.m.
Barnett, Kerry—Center for Study of Responsive Law, 202/387-8030, 6/2, 10:25; 6/3, 11:55; 7/8, 11:15 & 4:43; 6/18, 10:30.
Bartlett, Helen—Mich. Dept. of Atty. Genl., Charitable Trust Section, 517/373-1152, 6/4, 10:48.
Barton, Carol—Better Business Bureau, 202/393-8000, 6/16, 2:45; 6/18, 2:00.
Beasly, Ray—Consumer Protection, Louisiana, 504/925-4401.

Bell, Judy—Consumer Protection Division, New Hampshire, 603/271-3591, 603/224-5500.

Berliner, David—Assoc. Dir., Consumers Union, 914/664-6400, 6/30, 3:55.

Blackman, Ruth—Librarian, Gannett News Service, 202/862-4900, 5/28, 11:00 a.m.

Bolger, Bill—National Resource Center for Consumers of Legal Services, 202/659-8514, 7/3 & 8/15, 2:25.

Bray, Howard—Fund for Investigative Journalism, 202/462-1844, 7/3.

Brewster, Tish—Asst. Dir., Center for Science in the Public Interest, 202/332-9110, 7/3.

Bridgeforth, Mrs.—Balt. IRS, 301/566-5000, 5/22, 11:45 a.m.

Brown, Don—Deputy Atty. Genl., Delaware, 302/571-4221.

Brownstein, Ron—Center for Study of Responsive Law, 202/387-8030, 5/21, 4:25 p.m.; 5/27, 4:50; 6/3, 10:50.

Butler, Lejoie—Center for Woman Policy Studies, 202/872-1770, 8/15, 3:55.

California Citizen Action Group—213/475-0417, 7/9-11, 8/14.

Campbell, Larry—Registrar of Charitable Trusts, Dept. of Justice, California, 916/445-2021.

Caple, Velma—Secy. of State's Office, Arkansas, 501/370-5166.

Carlson, Richard—Center for Study of Responsive Law, 202/387-8030, 6/20, 11:40.

Cate, Margery—Charitable Solicitations Coordinator, Dept. of State, Div. of Licensing, Florida, 904/488-5381.

Centrileure, JoAnne—Corporations Dept., Secy. of State, Kansas, 913/296-2236.

Chapman, Jane—Dir., Center for Woman Policy Studies, 202/872-1770, 6/26, 3:30.

Claffey, Connie—Washington Legal Foundation, 202/827-0240, 7/22, 4:40.

Clovis, Deborah—Council for Public Interest Law, 202/624-8390, 7/3.

Cook, Larry—D.C. Tax Registration, 727-6130, 7/18, 9:30.

Cooper, Jill—Atty. Genl.'s Office, New Mexico, 505/827-5521.

Corbin, Robert—Atty. Genl., Arizona, 602/255-4266.

Cozzens, Mr.—N.Y. Charities Office, 518/473-8153, 6/12, 9:15 a.m., 6/18, 2:15.

DiPietro, Linda—Consumer Protection Fraud Division, Connecticut, 203/566-3035.

Dubill, Bob—Exec. Ed., Gannett News Service, 202/862-4900, 7/7, 11:50.

de Toledano, Ralph—202/638-1037, 6/23, 4:30.

Edgarton, Ed.—Solicitation Licensing Branch, Dept. of Human Resources, North Carolina, 919/733-4510.

Ettinger, Debra—N.J. PIRG, 609/393-7474, 8/14, 5:40 p.m.

Fazzolari, Karen—Pa. Commission on Charitable Organizations, 717/783-1720, 6/4, 10:15 a.m.

Ferguson, Karen—Dir., Pension Rights Center, 202/296-3778, 7/14.

Field, Myrna—Mid-Atlantic Legal Foundation, 215/545-1913, 5/29, 4:05 p.m.; 6/4, 8:55.

Finigan, Pat—Secy. of State's Office, Maine, 207/289-3501.

Fiorello, Kathy—Tax Reform Research Group, 202/544-1710, 7/9.

Foster, Liz—Council of Better Business Bureaus, Inc., 202/862-1200, 6/18, 2:10.

Furth, Lesley—Fund for Constitutional Government, 202/546-3732, 7/3.

Galvin, John—Secy. of State's Office, Iowa, 515/281-5204.

Garlow, Charlie—Co-Dir., Americans Concerned About Corporate Power [Big Business Day], 202/861-0456, 7/7; 8/14, 4:45.

Glassman, Jonathan—National Coordinator, Gray Panthers, 215/382-3300, 8/14, 4:35.

Goldberg, Michael—Professional Drivers Council, 202/785-3707, 7/3, 3:49.

Goidrey, Bill—Review of the News, Inc., 617/489-0600, 6/26, 9:05.

Grossman Publishers, 212/755-4330, 6/27, 10:05.

Grossman Publishers, 202/785-4073, 7/9-11.

Hancock, Don—Dir., S.W. Research & Information Center, 505/242-4766, 7/9, 3:15 p.m.; 8/14, 5:30.

Hanon, Ellis—Asst. Atty. Genl., Alabama, 205/832-5936.

Harvey, Ann—Fraser Associates, 202/452-1188, 6/17, 11:35 a.m.; 6/23, 4:20.

Hickey, Roger—Consumers Opposed to Inflation in the Necessaries, 202/833-3208, 7/3.

Hitchcock, Corn—Transportation Consumer Action Project, 202/223-0287, 7/7.

Hopkins, Bruce—Commercial lawyer, 1010 Wisconsin Ave., N.W., Washington, D.C.

Hopper, Jean—Gray Panthers, 215/382-3300, 7/3, 2:10.

Horrocks, Mike—Public Citizen Visitors Center, 202/543-4404, 6/2, 3:50; 6/3, 11:20; 6/12, 10:00; 6/27, 9:55; interview 6/5; 8/15, 12:20.

Houston, John—Public Service Research Council, 6/10, 9:40 a.m., 4:40.

Ingram, Miss—*Washington Post* Advertising Dept., 202/334-6130, 6/27, 10:50 a.m.

Jamir, Karla—Monsour Medical Foundation; 202/462-0505, 7/1-3.

Jamir, Karla—Comm. for the Advancement of Public Interest Organizations, 6/26, 11:50.

Jester, Harvey—Accountant, Public Safety Research Institute, The Rosewater Foundation, Safety Systems Foundation, 203/536-9402, 202/452-4817, 7/8, 9:58; 7/9, 10:41; 8/14.

Johnson, Willa—Heritage Foundation, 202/546-4400, 5/20.

Kavasharou, Sarah—Asst. Atty. Genl., Alaska, 907/465-3960.

Lang, Helen—Secy. to Deputy Secy. of State, Nebraska, 402/471-2554.

Little, Faith—Center for Auto Safety, Inc., 202/659-1126, 7/2.

Lucas, Cicero—Secy. of State's Office, Georgia, 404/656-2859.

Mancini, John—Foundation for Public Affairs, Research Department, 202/872-1750, 7/2, 4:30.

Marshall, Joe—Mid-Atlantic Legal Foundation, 8/14, 10:50 a.m.; 6/17, 9:45.

Masters, Rick—Asst. Atty. Genl., Kentucky, 502/564-6607.

McCrainey, Ms. —Gannett News Service, 202/862-4900, 5/28, 10:20.

McKennan, Jennifer—Equal Justice Foundation, 202/452-1267, 6/26 4:00 p.m.

Meth, Buddy—Dir., Accountants for the Public Interest, 212/575-1828, 2/9/80.

Minyard, Chuck—Consumer Protection, Louisiana, 504/425-4401.

Mississippi Attorney General's Office, 601/354-7130.

Mlinar, Jan—Commerce Dept., Securities Division, Minnesota, 612/296-4522.

Moore, Carolyn—Center for Women Policy Studies, 202/872-1770, 6/26, 2:00 p.m.

Mott of Washington & Assoc, —202/785-1445, 7/9-11.

Nagota, Russell—Business Registration Div., Dept. of Regulatory Agencies.

Palmer, Carol—N.Y. State Office of Charities Registration, 518/474-3720, 6/4, 9:30; 6/9, 12:01 p.m.

Pendergrass, Jane—National Information Bureau, Inc., 212/532-8595, 6/16, 2:35 p.m.

Philanthropic Advisory Service of the Council of Better Busines Bureaus, 202/862-1228, 6/16, 3:00 p.m.

Pollack, Richard—Dir., Critical Mass Energy Project, 202/546-4790, 7/8, 5:40.

Rapoport, Miles—Dir., Conn. Citizens Action Group, 203/527-7191, 7/8/80, 3:18 p.m., 8/14, 12:35.

Richards, Joseph—Dir., Dept. of Licenses Business Licensing, Investigations & Inspections, 202/727-3645, 6/10, 9:55; 6/27, 10:30.

Riley, Jim—Inheritance Tax Division, Office of Atty. Genl., Colo., 303/839-2381.

Rosen, Joel—Office of Atty. Genl., Illinois, 312/793-2595.

Rosmeyre, Susan—Secy. of State's Office, Indiana, 317/232-6531.

Rossman, Vern—Exec. Dir., Accountants for the Public Interest, 212/732-1475, 8/14, 3:00 p.m.

Rubin, Sidney—Head Accountant, N.Y. State Bureau of Charities, 212/488-7456, 6/12, 9:50 a.m.; 6/18, 11:40.

Sadler—IRS Public Inspection Unit, Philadelphia, 215/969-2446, 7/7, 2:50 p.m.

Salustro, Larry—Asst. Atty. Genl., Minnesota, 612/296-6438.

Sanford, David—Harper's, 212/481-5247, 6/4, 9:50 a.m.

Sarah—Public Citizen Visitor's Center, 202/543-4404, 6/17, 4:40 p.m.

Schwartz, Frieda—Fraser Assoc., 202/452-1188, 6/27, 10:10.

Shimshack, Rachael—Congress Watch, 202/543-5123, 7/8/80.

Simon, Ruth—Info. Officer, Consumer Federation of America, 202/737-3732, 7/7/80; 8/15/80, 4:00 p.m.

Singer, Jim—*National Journal*, 202/857-1400, 6/3, 2:45.

Singleton, Julia—Massachusetts Dir. of Public Charities, 617/727-2235, 6/4, 10:25 a.m.

Smith, Bob—*N.Y. Times* Ad Acceptability, 212/354-3900, 6/26, 8:55.

Smith, Emmy—Accountant, Center for Study of Responsive Law, 202/387-8030, 6/2, 3:55; 6/3, 10:40.

Snyder, Karen—Disability Rights Center, 202/273-3304, 7/3/80; 8/15, 3:05.

Sprigg, Sherry—Secy. of State's Office, Montana, 314/751-3321.

Stahman, Myrna—Office of Atty. Genl., Idaho, 208/334-2400.

Stankyo, David—Legislative Counsel Bureau, Nevada, 702/885-5627.

Steinberg, Gary—Clean Water Action Project, 202/638-1196, 6/25, 11:35 a.m.

Suffern, Kevin—Dir. of Public Charities, Massachusetts, 617/727-2235.

Superintendant of Corporations—DC Recorder of Deeds, 202/727-5208, 6/4, 9:20 a.m.

Sweeney, Louise—*Christian Science Monitor*, 202/785-4400, 5/28, 10:35 a.m.

Swenson, Frank—N.J. Charities Registration Section, 201/648-4002, 6/4, 9:45 a.m.

Thal, Lorraine—Freedom of Information Clearinghouse, 202/785-3704, 7/8, 4:47 p.m.; 7/9, 10:00 a.m.

Tulman, Joe—Asst. Dir., Equal Justice Foundation, 202/452-1267, 7/3, 4:00 p.m.

Utzig, Holly—Conn. Citizen Action Group, 203/527-7191, 6/26, 2:10.

Valentine—D.C. Dept. of Licenses, Investigations & Inspections, Office of Licenses & Permits, Business Licensing Branch, 202/727-3645, 5/22, 11:45.

Vladeck, David—Public Citizen Litigation Group, 202/785-3704, 7/8/80.

Waldbauer, Kathy—Aviation Consumer Action Project, 6/26, 11:00 a.m.

Wathen, Tom—N.Y. PIRG, 212/349-6460, 8/15, 3:42.

Waz, Joe—Deputy. Dir., National Citizens Comm. for Broadcasting, 202/462-2520, 6/30, 4:05.

Weaver—Office of Charitable Contributions, Maryland, 301/269-3421.

Weeks, Nancy—Secy. of State's Office, Missouri, 314/751-3321.

Wetherill, Phyllis—"D.E.S. Registry," 202/966-1766, 8/14, 2:56.

Wolfe, Dr. Samuel—Director, Health-Research Group, 202/872-0320. 7/9, 2:49.

Zill, Anne—President, Fund for Constitutional Government, 7/7/70, 8/15, 3:40.

Appendix C
The Nader Network:
Primary and
Subgroups

Listed below are the 19 primary organizations and subgroups that make up the Nader network. The listings include address, date of incorporation or founding, tax status, purpose and activities. In alphabetical order, the groups are:

Americans Concerned about Corporate Power

Address: 1346 Connecticut Ave., N.W., 411 and 1126, 16th Street, N.W., Washington, D.C. 20036.

Incorporated: 7/24/79 in D.C.

Tax Status: Exempt under IRC Section 501 (c) (3).

Purpose: "To inform the public about the influence of corporations on American society, alternatives to traditional corporations, and any other issue relating to the American economy."[1]

Activities: ACACP is a coalition of "50 or 60" organizations "concerned about abuses of corporate power and the insensitivity of corporations to needs of the community.[2] It organized "Big Business Day" on April 17, 1980, to "expose and repair big business." A legislative goal of the Day was passage of a proposed "Corporate Democracy Act," which "would grant greater rights and access and voice to the various constituencies of the giant corporation—workers, consumers, communities, and shareholders."[3] ACACP continues to work on other projects "along the same line" and is considering the possibility of sponsoring an annual "Big Business Day."[4]

ACACP is otherwise known as the Big Business Day Committee. Mr. Nader was an "Initiating Sponsor" of the committee and serves as a member of its board of advisors.

Aviation Consumer Action Project

Address:	1346 Connecticut Ave., N.W., 717, Washington, D.C. 20036.
Incorporated:	4/19/71 in D.C. as the "Aviation Consumer Advocacy Project." Name amended to its present form on 3/31/72.
Tax Status:	Originally tax-exempt under IRC Section 501 (c) (4). Now exempt under Section 501 (c) (3).
Purpose:	"Educational and charitable activities in support of safety and consumer interests in aviation."[5]
Activities:	"Activities include distributing passenger information leaflets and advocacy of passenger interests before federal regulatory agencies and the courts. Seeks: lower fares and increased competition in domestic and international air transportation; im-

proved airline crash survivability; elimination of unfair consumer practices; open government." Publishes newsletters and a pamphlet entitled "Facts and Advice for Airline Passengers.[6]

Mr. Nader has been "closely involved with ACAP since the beginning," said an ACAP spokesman.[7] He serves as the Chairman of ACAP's Advisory Board, upon which ACAP places "strong reliance for advice."[8]

Mimi Cutler serves as President of ACAP. ACAP has a full-time staff of four, plus a varying number of interns and volunteers.

Center for the Study of Responsive Law

Address:	P.O. Box 19367, Washington, D.C. 20036. Street address is unavailable.[9]
Founded:	6/28/68 as a charitable trust in D.C.
Tax Status:	Exempt under IRC Section 501 (c) (3).
Purpose:	"To engage in, sponsor, encourage and disseminate research studies, educational programs, publications and other types of educational materials relating to the general question of the responsiveness of law and legal institutions to the needs of the public, including problems regarding citizen access to the legislative, judicial and executive branches of government.[10]
Activities:	CSRL's activities are limited to "purely research," according to accountant Emmy Smith.[11] Mike Horrocks, director of Public Citizen's Visitors Center, described CSRL as "Nader's Brookings Institute," a "think

tank," . . . where our general philosophies emanate.[12] CSRL operates the Freedom Information Clearinghouse (see below) and the "Diffusion Project," which "diffuse[s] information on social change innovations to people who might want to implement similar reforms."[13] It also operates the Learning Research Project and Citizens Utility Board. More specific information about the activities of the Center was unavailable.

The Center for Study of Responsive Law, the first generally publicized Nader organization, was formed as a charitable trust in Washington, D.C., on June 28, 1968. Mr. Nader was the sole founding trustee. Theodore Jacobs, a close associate of Mr. Nader for several years thereafter, served as Trust Settlor[14] and as the Center's first executive director. Sheila Harty is currently listed as Administrator of the Center.[15] Mr. Nader controls the Center as Managing Trustee.[16]

The Center was established as a tax-exempt organization under Section 501 (c) (3) of the Internal Revenue Code of 1954, and can therefore attract contributions which are tax deductible. Its activities may not, however, include a "substantial" amount of lobbying.[17]

Consequently, the Center operates primarily as a research and educational organization. The Center has served as the major source of Nader study group reports, of which at least 18 were published between 1969 and 1974. As Mr. Nader's strategy has shifted from using research and exposés to working actively for reforms, the number of reports issued by the Center has declined.

No further information is available about the activities of the Center for Study of Responsive Law. Because of the secrecy of the Center, the current subjects of their research remain chiefly unknown. We could not even find out how large the Center's staff is. Kerry Barnett, who identified himself as "Front Office Manager" of the Center and "assistant" to Mr. Nader, stated that he did not know the number of Center employees.[18] Mr. Barnett also refused to disclose the Center's street address.[19]

Citizen Utility Board

Address:	P.O. Box 19312, Washington, D.C. 20036.
Founded:	1979 in Washington, D.C.
Purpose:	"CUB will be a state-wide organization of citizens fighting to protect their interests as residential utility consumers. . . . CUB will give individual consumers an efficient way to pool small amounts of money, time and ideas to challenge utility company waste and greed."[20]
Activities:	"CUB will make sure there are accountants, lawyers, economists and engineers working for the consumer. It will make sure that state regulatory commissions and other public bodies hear both sides of a case. CUB will insure that the utilities' rate increase requests receive a thorough and independent analysis."[21]

CUB is a project of the Center for Study of Responsive Law. On 11/28/79, Wisconsin became the first state to enact a CUB bill. "Citizens in more than a dozen states have pushed their state legislatures to consider CUB bills."[22]

Congress Watch

Address:	215 Penn. Ave., S.E., Washington, D.C. 20003.
Founded:	1973 in D.C.
Tax Status:	Not applicable; Congress Watch is a dependent subgroup of Public Citizen.
Purpose:	"Is the research and advocacy arm of Public Citizen on Capitol Hill."[23]
Activities:	Congress Watch's recent lobbying efforts have promoted the strengthening of the Freedom of Information Act; the facilitating of "consumer" representation before the FTC; the abolition of the Joint Committee on Atomic Energy; and the enactment of the National Consumer Cooperative Bank Act.[24] Congress Watch also issues reports and publishes *The Congress Watcher* newsletter. Congress Watch began organizing "Congress Watch Locals" in 1979 "to amplify its voice in Congress."[25] By March 1980, there were Locals in 26 Congressional Districts throughout the country.[26]

Congress Watch was founded in 1973 as the congressional lobbying division of Public Citizen. Nancy Drabble has served as acting director since Mark Green resigned his position as director in Spring 1980 to run for Congress. Congress Watch currently has a full-time staff of approximately 14.[27]

Corporate Accountability Research Group

Address:	1346 Connecticut Ave., N.W., 419A, Washington, D.C. 20036.
Founded:	1972 or 1973 in D.C.[28]

Tax Status: CARG is not listed in IRS files as tax-exempt.[29]

Purpose: "The chief mission of the Corporate Accountability Research Group is to draft—and lobby for—Nader's . . . federal chartering scheme [for corporations] CARG was originally established to follow through on the findings of Nader's antitrust investigation."[30]

Activities: Publishes the *Multinational Monitor,* a magazine with "reporting and analysis each month on the activities of . . . giant [multinational] corporations and the governmental and citizen responses to their growing power."[31] Publication of the *Monitor* is CARG's sole activity at present.[32]

CARG is closely connected with Mr. Nader's Public Interest Research Group. CARG and PIRG had a combined staff of six persons working together on the *Multinational Monitor* magazine, which investigates multinational corporations.[33]

CARG was originally founded as an outgrowth of the Nader antitrust study in the early 1970s.[34] It is funded by Mr. Nader from his personal income. Its annual budget totaled approximately $50,000 in 1975;[35] more recent budget information is unavailable.

Critical Mass Energy Project

Address: 215 Penn. Ave., S.E. Washington, D.C. 20003.

Founded: 1974 in D.C.

Tax Status: Not applicable; CMEP is a dependent subgroup of Public Citizen.

Purpose: "To direct the public's attention to the fact that we at Public Citizen do not believe that nuclear energy is the right direction to go in."[36]

Activities: "CMEP has challenged nuclear industry propaganda concerning the cost, safety and need for nuclear power. The Project has fought for greater public participation in nuclear plant licensing, drawn attention to the high concentration of ownership in the nuclear industry and fought for improved emergency planning for nuclear accidents."[37]

CMEP grew out of a conference on nuclear energy, Critical Mass '74, sponsored by Public Citizen. CMEP has worked "not only to ensure that there is a halt to nuclear energy, but that renewable energy resources—solar, wind, ocean, hydro and geothermal energy—are allowed to blossom."[38] It has campaigned for greater public participation in nuclear plant licensing and fought for stronger governmental controls over the transportation of radioactive materials. CMEP has organized public rallies against nuclear energy, lobbied in Congress and petitioned the Nuclear Regulatory Commission. It publishes special reports, investigative studies, "Legislative Alerts," and "Action Alerts," as well as a monthly *Critical Mass Journal*. Richard Pollock is director of CMEP, which has a full-time staff of three.[39]

Equal Justice Foundation
Address: 1333 Connecticut Ave., N.W. Washington, D.C. 20036.

Incorporated: 8/7/78 in D.C.

Tax Status: Exempt under IRC Section 501 (c) (3).

Purpose: "To study and promote means by which citizens may enjoy access to representation in the courts, legislative bodies, administrative agencies and other governmental forums where public policies are made . . . ."[40]

Activities: "The Equal Justice Foundation is a membership organization of lawyers and law students dedicated to procedural and structural reform of the law. All work is aimed at increasing access of the under-represented to decision-making forums . . . . The agenda of reform includes liberalizing class action procedures, easing standing-to-sue requirements, increasing funding for citizen participation in agency proceedings, promoting statutes authorizing attorney fees compensation for public interest litigants, and encouraging the development of alternative dispute resolution mechanisms."[41]

The Foundation was founded by Mr. Nader, in cooperation with public interest lawyers and law students.[42] It is funded in part by tithing: law students are asked to pledge at least 1 percent of their annual postgraduate income. The "major source of funds" at present is the honoraria which Mr. Nader receives for speeches at law schools and donates to the Foundation.[43] The current chairman of the board is Steve Rosenbaum. Susan Kellock serves as executive director.

Freedom of Information Clearinghouse

Address:	2000 P Street, N.W. 700, Washington, D.C. 20036.
Founded:	1972 in Washington, D.C.
Tax Status:	Not applicable; the Clearinghouse is a dependent project operated by the Center for Study of Responsive Law.
Purpose:	The purpose of the Clearinghouse is to win release of documents from federal officials under the Freedom of Information Act.[44]
Activities:	"Its functions are to collect and disseminate information on state and federal Freedom of Information statutes; to assist citizens who seek information from the government; and to litigate a small number of cases generally chosen for their broad impact on case law."[45] The majority of those cases are reportedly brought on behalf of other Nader organizations.[46]

Health Research Group

Address:	2000 P Street, N.W. Suite 708, Washington, D.C. 20036.
Founded:	November 1971 in D.C.
Tax Status:	Not applicable; HRG is a dependent subgroup of Public Citizen.
Purpose:	"Two missions—Fighting for the public's health in Washington, and giving consumers more control over decisions which affect their health—define the work of Public Citizen's Health Research Group.[47]

Activities: HRG has worked "in the areas of food and drug regulation, workplace safety and health, medical device and product safety, and health care delivery."[48] HRG has lobbied for the ban on Red Dye No. 2, published guides for health consumers, and "Challenged the medical establishment by drawing public attention to unnecessary surgery, over-prescription of drugs, uncontrolled hospital expansions and the ill-advised purchase of expensive hospital equipment."[49] HRG has also engaged in litigation attempting to enforce health and safety regulations, and issued a large number of reports presenting results of HRG's research.

The Group was founded in November 1971, only eight months after the incorporation of Public Citizen. Sidney Wolfe, M.D., has served as HRG's Director since its inception. His staff currently numbers approximately nine persons.[50]

Learning Research Project
Address: P.O. Box 19312, Washington, D.C.
Founded: 1979 in Washington, D.C.[51]
Tax Status: Not applicable; the Project is a dependent subgroup of the Center for Study of Responsive Law.
Activities: The Learning Research Project published a report on the Educational Testing Service (ETS) in January 1980. It plans to continue work on "related issues."[53]

185

National Citizens Committee for Broadcasting

Address:	P.O. Box 12038, Washington, D.C. 20005.
Incorporated:	1967 in NY as "National Citizens Committee for Public Broadcasting." Re-incorporated 11/8/72 in D.C. under its present name.
Tax Status:	Exempt under IRC Section 501 (c) (3).
Purpose:	"a) To encourage widespread public interest in improving the performance of radio and television stations and other broad-band communication systems.
	b). To educate the public as to the standards and procedures to assess programming and legal means to bring about improved public service by broadcaster and other broad-band communications.
	c) To educate the public regarding the history and economics of broad-band communications and current issues affecting it.
	d) To assist community groups in legal actions to protect public rights."[53]
Activities:	"Engaged in assisting groups in gaining access to regulatory processes affecting broadcast media."[54]

Mr. Nader has served as the Chairman of NCCB's Board of Directors since October 1978.[55] The other two directors are Nicholas Johnson and Robert J. Stein. NCCB has approximately 8,000 members, primarily in the United States but also abroad.[56] Its staff consists of about six persons.

Public Citizen, Inc.

Address: 1346 Connecticut Avenue, N.W., 1209, Washington, D.C. 20036.

Incorporated: 3/29/71 in D.C.

Tax Status: Exempt under IRC Section 501 (c) (4).

Purpose: "To promote, encourage and foster the common good and general welfare of the people of the United States through bringing about civic betterments and social improvements. . . . To promote, encourage and foster citizen involvement in government and other public processes by which social decisions are made. . . . To promote, encourage and foster the establishment of organizations of lawyers and other professional persons working in the public interest to aid citizen involvement in, and to conduct research into, such areas as governmental responsiveness, consumer protection, corporate responsibility, protection of the environment, and civil liberties and civil rights."[57]

Activities: "Public Citizen's programs for the Eighties will emphasize the instruments of citizen cooperation around specific issues and the creation of opportunities for participation by citizens in government and other forums where large corporations shape power or dictate their will." Those "specific issues" include energy, inflation, tax abuse, product hazards, pollution, health and safety, and government and corporate accountability.[58]

Although the Nader-funded Public Interest Research Group was originally intended to serve as the "action" group for Nader projects, a wider funding base was eventually needed as Mr. Nader placed still heavier emphasis upon lobbying activities. With the incorporation of Public Citizen in 1971, Mr. Nader began to appeal directly to the American public for financial support.

Public Citizen's direct-mail solicitation efforts requesting small contributions from thousands of citizens, have succeeded in raising approximately $1 million each year since Public Citizen's incorporation. Since Public Citizen is classified as a 501 (c) (4) organization under the Internal Revenue Code of 1954, these contributions are not tax-deductible.

Public Citizen is, however, permitted, as a 501 (c) (4) organization, to engage in lobbying. It has consequently become Mr. Nader's most active and most highly-publicized organization.

Public Citizen currently funds and operates six subgroups, each of which conducts activities of its own in accordance with Public Citizen's general purpose. Although each subgroup has an executive director, their activities are clearly controlled by Mr. Nader in his capacity as president,[59] treasurer and director of Public Citizen. Each of the six groups works independently of the others and is "responsible only to Mr. Nader."[60]

The six Public Citizen subgroups are: Congress Watch, Critical Mass Energy Project, Health Research Group, Tax Reform Research Group, Litigation Group, and the Visitors Center.

Public Citizen Litigation Group
Address: 2000 P Street, N.W. 700, Washington, D.C. 20036.

Founded: 1972 in D.C.

Tax Status: Not applicable; the Litigation Group is a dependent subgroup of Public Citizen.

Purpose: "The Litigation Group is the courtroom arm of Public Citizen, handling a variety of cases on behalf of consumers, workers and interested citizens."[61]

Activities: "Since the foundation in 1972, one of the group's principal focuses has been on making the professions more competitive and more responsive to consumers . . . . The Group has also been very active on health and safety issues, as they affect workers and consumers. Attacking government lawlessness has also been a major concern of the Group . . . . Together with the Freedom of Information Clearinghouse, it has been a major force in obtaining precedent-setting decisions releasing documents under the Freedom of Information Act."[62] The Litigation Group also "provides legal representation to other Nader groups."[63]

Alan B. Morrison serves as director, with a staff of nine lawyers and four support staff.[64] The Litigation Group shares offices with the Center of Responsive Law's Freedom of Information Clearinghouse.

Public Citizen Visitors Center

Address: 215 Penn. Ave., S.E. Washington, D.C. 20003.

Founded: 1973 in D.C.

Tax Status: Not applicable; the Center is a dependent subgroup of Public Citizen.

Purpose: "To provide visitors to the nation's

capitol a more meaningful look at their government."[65]

Activities: The center maintains an office which disseminates information about Public Citizen and other "public interest" groups. Visitors Center interns conduct guided tours of the capitol's buildings, arranges seminars on consumerism, and sponsors a public "Forum," "whose aim is to provide an open session where consumers can discuss their concerns with major federal government officials."[66] The Center also issues a bi-monthly newsletter, "Inside the Capitol."[67]

The Director of the Visitors Center is Mike Horrocks. The Center has a staff of three, supplemented by volunteer interns from colleges across the country.

Public Interest Research Group

Address: 1346 Connecticut Ave., N.W., 415, Washington, D.C. 20036.

Founded: 1970 in Washington, D.C.

Tax Status: Unavailable.

Purpose: Unavailable.

Activities: The PIRG group at 1346 Connecticut Avenue is currently working on "banking issues" and on the *Multinational Monitor*, a magazine published by the Corporate Accountability Research Group.[68]

As Mr. Nader's emphasis changed from research to action, he found it necessary to establish an organization which, unlike the Center for Study of Responsive Law, could engage in lobbying for reform. In 1970, therefore, Mr. Nader created the Public Interest Research Group (PIRG) with funds from his personal income. "Its job was . . . to induce federal administrative agencies, the courts, and Congress to adopt new policies by filing lawsuits, submitting petitions, and conducting lobbying campaigns."[69]

In order to promote "grass-roots" activity of this sort, Mr. Nader and his PIRG staffers soon began working to establish PIRG branches on college campuses across the country. A new organization, the Citizen Action Group, was founded in 1970 to help establish and coordinate the local public interest groups. By 1972, PIRG had been established in 17 states.

There are currently 175 active PIRG chapters in at least 30 states.[70] They are loosely coordinated by the National PIRG Clearinghouse, which was established by Mr. Nader in 1974 for that purpose.[71] The PIRG Clearinghouse was originally funded by Mr. Nader personally.[72] It also received a grant from the Center for Study of Responsive Law in 1978, although it allegedly operates independently of Mr. Nader now.

Each PIRG branch is funded independently by the students on its campus. The vast majority, if not all, of the PIRGs collect student dues through a "negative checkoff" system, proposed by Mr. Nader in his PIRG organizing manual, *Action for a Change.*[73] The procedure has become quite controversial of late. Three students are, in fact, now challenging the constitutionality of the PIRG checkoff in a case pending before the U.S. District of Court for the District of New Jersey.[74]

Mr. Nader has, for some reason, formally dissociated himself from all of the local PIRG branches since helping to form them. Mr. Nader's PIRG group claims that it is completely autonomous of the National PIRG Clearinghouse and the rest of the PIRG branches.

There are "no common projects or informational connections," said a Nader-PIRG spokesman.[75]

The Project Director of the National PIRG Clearinghouse, David Sand, confirmed that Mr. Nader is no longer connected, legally or financially, with the national or local PIRGs. "He exerts only spiritual control," Mr. Sand stated, adding, however, that Mr. Nader's Public Citizen, Inc., does provide the PIRGs with "help on issues and projects, and with information, etc."[76]

One of the "projects" with which Public Citizen is currently helping, we discovered, is the pending case brought against the New Jersey Rutgers PIRG by three Rutgers students.[77] A staff attorney with Public Citizen's Litigation Group, John Cary Sims, has been specially admitted to appear and participate in all proceedings of the case on behalf of NJPIRG.[78]

Furthermore, we discovered, a number of prominent Nader employees have left their posts at organizations directly controlled by Mr. Nader to join the New York branch of PIRG. The current Executive Director of NYPIRG, Mr. Donald Ross, is an ex-director of the Citizen Action Group. More recently, Kerry Barnett, front office manager at the Center for Study of Responsive Law, joined NYPIRG's Binghamton, N.Y., branch in the summer of 1980.

Although reportedly no longer connected with the PIRGs,[79] the Center for the Study of Responsive Law has a staff writer currently engaged in updating the PIRG organizing manual, *Action for a Change* (which was originally written in 1971 by Mr. Nader and Donald Ross).[80] In addition, Mr. Nader himself still gives speeches for PIRGs occasionally.[81]

Thus, even though there apparently exist no current legal or financial ties between Mr. Nader and the

PIRG branches, it is obvious that all connections between the two have not yet been completely severed.

Mr. Nader's original PIRG group still exists as such, currently working on banking issues and on publication of the *Multinational Monitor* magazine, which investigates the activities of multinational corporations. Its staff, which once included over a dozen attorneys,[82] now numbers two.[83] Mr. Nader "runs the Research group because he pays the salaries," said PIRG's office manager.[84] Funding for the Group comes from Mr. Nader's personal income.[85] PIRG has no directors or trustees.[86]

Public Safety Research Institute

Address: 3900 N. Upland Street, Arlington, VA 22207.

Incorporated: 3/13/68 in Delaware.

Tax Status: Exempt under IRC Section 501 (c) (3).

Purpose: "To undertake, promote, develop and carry on religious, charitable, scientific, literary, or educational work; to establish and maintain in whole or in part religious, charitable, scientific, literary, or educational agencies or institutions; in the absolute discretion of the Board of Trustees, to make donations, gifts, contributions and loans. . . ."[87]

The Institute was the second Nader organization to be established, preceding the formation of the Center for the Study of Responsive Law by three months. Mr. Nader serves as president and treasurer of the Institute and as one of its three directors. Mr. Nader's cousins from Toronto, Edmund and Diana Shaker, are the other two directors.[88]

Due to the relatively lax disclosure requirements for Delaware corporations—requirements Mr. Nader has sharply criticized[89]—little is known about the actual activities of the Public Safety Research Institute. Its sole activity, as far as we could determine, has been to make grants to other organizations, many of which have been controlled by Mr. Nader.

Safety Systems Foundation

Address:	3900 N. Upland Street, Arlington, VA 22207.
Founded:	11/7/66 in N.Y. as a trust.
Tax Status:	Exempt under IRC Section 501 (c) (3).
Purpose:	"This trust is created and shall be operated exclusively for religious, charitable, scientific, literary, or educational purposes, or for the prevention of cruelty to children or animals, within the United States or any of its possessions."[90]
Activities:	"The trust has no business activities but is engaged solely in charitable, educational and scientific activities, namely, the sponsoring of research projects and the dissemination of information as well as the making of grants to charities qualified within the meaning of Section 501 (c) (3) of the IRC of 1954."[91]

The little-publicized Safety Systems Foundation was the first Nader organization, predating the Center for Study of Responsive Law by almost two years. It was formed on November 11, 1966, as a charitable trust under the laws of New York.

Theodore Jacobs, a close associate of Mr. Nader for a number of years, was the Trust Settlor for Safety

Systems. Mrs. Laura Nader Milleron, sister of Ralph Nader, was and still is the sole Trustee. Mr. Nader has been the sole contributor of Safety Systems each year since its formation.

The Foundation's sole activity, according to available information, has thus far been to make a small number of grants to other organizations, most of which have been controlled directly by Mr. Nader.

Tax Reform Research Group

Address:	215 Penn. Ave., S.E. Washington, D.C. 20003.
Founded:	1972 in D.C.
Tax Status:	Not applicable; the Research Group is a dependent subgroup of Public Citizen.
Purpose:	"Works in Congress, monitors the Internal Revenue Service and assists local groups around the country to advance progressive tax reform."[92]
Activities:	". . . TRRG has worked closely with local groups to fight tax proposals which inhibit genuine reform and give tax relief largely to corporations and wealthy individuals. By the same token, TRRG has strongly supported state and local efforts advancing progressive tax measures, including property tax assessment reforms, progressive property tax relief, and repeal of sales taxes on food and medicine. In addition to these activities, TRRG publishes *People & Taxes* each month. . . ."[93]

Robert McIntyre serves as director, with a staff of three.[94]

NOTES

1. Articles of Incorporation.

2. Statement by Charlie Garlow, Co-director of ACACP—phone conversation, 7/7/80.

3. Press release issued by Big Business Day—6 p.m., Wednesday, December 12, 1979.

4. Statement by Charlie Garlow—phone conversation, 8/14/80.

5. Statement of affairs conducted in D.C., filed with the D.C. Corporate Records Office—Annual Report, 1/25/78.

6. *Encyclopedia of Associations,* vol. 1, 14th ed., eds., Nancy Yakes and Denise Akey (Detroit: Gale Research Co., 1980). Original copyright, 1959.

7. Statement by Kathy Waldbauer, Administrative Assistant— phone conversation, 6/26/80.

8. Ibid.

9. Mr. Kerry Barnett, "front office manager" of the Center for Study of Responsive Law and "assistant to Mr. Nader"—phone conversation, July 8, 1980.

10. Trust agreement.

11. Phone conversation, 6/3/80.

12. Interview, 6/5/80.

13. Letter by Nader in the *Diffusion* newsletter (undated issue distributed at Public Citizen's Visitors Center as of May 23, 1980).

14. As of June 28, 1968, when the Trust Agreement was signed between Jacobs and Nader, the Center had no assets. There are no reports of Jacobs subsequently donating funds to the Center. He is, nevertheless, the legal settlor of the trust.

15. *Encyclopedia of Associations,* vol. 1, 14th ed.

16. Susan Gross, "The Nader Network," in *Business and Society Review*, vol. 13 (1975), p. 5.

17. See earlier section on tax status.

18. Kerry Barnett—phone conversation, July 8, 1980.

19. Ibid.

20. CUB literature available at Public Citizen's Visitors Center as of 5/23/80.

21. Ibid.

22. Ibid.

23. Public Citizen's 1979 Annual Report.

24. Ibid.

25. Ibid.

26. *The Congress Watcher*, March/April 1980, p. 10 (published by Public Citizen's Congress Watch).

27. Statement by Rachael Shimshack, Congress Watch Office Manager—phone conversation, 7/8/80.

28. Statement by Mike Horrocks—phone conversation, 8/18/80.

29. Letter of 8/6/80 from D. Sadler of IRS.

30. Susan Gross, "The Nader Network," p. 14.

31. *Multinational Monitor*, April 1980, vol. 1, No. 3.

32. Statement by Marilyn Osterman, PIRG/CARG Office Manager—phone conversation, 7/8/80.

33. Statement by Marilyn Osterman, PIRG/CARG Office Manager—phone conversation, 7/8/80.

34. Susan Gross, "The Nader Network," p. 14.

35. Ibid.

36. Statement by Mike Horrocks—phone conversation, 8/18/80.

37. Public Citizen's 1979 Annual Report.

38. Richard Pollock, "Working for a Safe Energy Future," *The Public Citizen*, Winter 1980 p. 2.

39. Statement by Richard Pollock, Director of CMEP—phone conversation, 7/8/80.

40. Articles of Incorporation.

41. Letter dated 7/14/80 from EJF, re: Law Conference for Legal Interns.

42. "Nader," Virginia Law Weekly, *DICTA*. vol. 32, No. 24 (1980), p. 1.

43. Statement by Jennifer McKenna, Office Manager and Researcher at EJF—phone conversation, 6/26/80.

44. Susan Gross, "The Nader Network," p. 9.

45. Statement mailed upon request to Capital Legal Foundation by Lorraine Thal of the Clearinghouse, received 7/11/80.

46. Susan Gross, "The Nader Network," p. 9.

47. Public Citizen's 1979 Annual Report.

48. Letter by Sidney Wolfe, M.D. (Director of HRG), in the November 1979 brochure describing its publishing.

49. Public Citizen's 1979 Annual Report.

50. "Profile" (published by the Washington, D.C., Foundation for Public Affairs), 4/1/79.

51. Statement by Mike Horrocks—phone conversation, 8/18/80.

52. Ibid.

53. Articles of Incorporation.

54. Statement of affairs conducted in D.C. filed with D.C. Corporate Records Office, 4/16/79, Annual Report.

55. Statement by Joe Waz, Deputy Director of NCCB—phone conversation, 6/30/80.

56. Ibid.

57. Articles of Incorporation.

58. *The Public Citizen,* Winter 1980, p. 1 (published by Public Citizen, Inc.); Public Citizen's 1979 Annual Report.

59. Nader no longer holds this position, having resigned last fall. Dr. Sidney Wolfe, head of the Health Research Group, was made President of Public Citizen upon Nader's resignation. "Ralph Nader Resigns from Consumer Post," Washington Post, 10/28/80.

60. Statement by Mike Horrocks, Director of Public Citizen's Visitors Center—interview, 6/5/80.

61. Public Citizen's 1979 Annual Report.

62. Ibid.

63. Statement by David Vladeck of the Litigation Group—phone conversation, 7/8/80.

64. Statement by David Vladeck of PCLG—phone conversation, 7/8/80.

65. Public Citizen's 1979 Annual Report.

66. Ibid.

67. Ibid.

68. Statement by Marilyn Osterman, Office Manager of PIRG/CART—phone conversation, 7/8/80.

69. Susan Gross, "The Nader Network," in *Business and Society Review,* vol. 13, 1975, p. 5.

70. Statement by Robin Ferber, Project Coordinator of National PIRG—phone conversation, 7/8/80.

71. Susan Gross, "The Nader Network," in *Business and Society Review,* vol. 13, 1975, p. 6.

72. Ibid.

73. Co-authored with Donald Ross. (New York: Grossman Publishers, 1971). Revised ed., 1972.

74. *Galda et al.* v. *Bloustein et al.* Civil Action No. 79-2811, pending before the U.S. District Court for the District of New Jersey.

75. Marilyn Osterman, PIRG Office Manager—phone conversation, 7/8/80.

76. Phone conversation, 7/2/80.

77. *Galda et al.* v. *Bloustein et al.* Civil Action No. 79-2811.

78. Ordered by the Honorable Stanley S. Brotman, United States District Judge.

79. Statement by Mike Horrocks, Director of Public Citizen's Visitors Center—interview, 6/5/80.

80. Statement by Annie at the Center for Study of Responsive Law—phone conversation, 6/27/80.

81. Statement by Mike Horrocks, Director of Public Citizen's Visitors Center—interview, 6/5/80.

82. Susan Gross, "The Nader Network," in *Business and Society Review*, vol. 13, 1975, p. 5.

83. Statement by Marilyn Osterman, Office Manager of PIRG/CART—phone conversation, 7/8/80.

84. Ibid.

85. Statement by Mike Horrocks, Director of Public Citizen's Visitors Center—interview, 6/5/80.

86. Statement by Marilyn Osterman, PIRG Office Manager—phone conversation, 7/8/80.

87. Public Safety Research Institute Articles of Incorporation.

88. Barbara O'Reilley, "Nader Series," written for Gannett News Service, 3/30/79.

89. See, for example: *The Company State;* Nader's study group report on Dupont in Delaware, by James Phelan and Robert Pozen (Grossman New York), 1973.

90. Trust agreement.

91. Form 990-A filed by Safety Systems with the IRS in 1967.

92. Public Citizen's 1979 Annual Report.

93. Ibid.

94. Answer to questionnaire sent by Capital Legal Foundation to the Tax Reform Research Group.

Appendix D
Other Groups Connected
with the Network

Pursuant to Chapter 4, additional details about organizations that have or had discernible ties to Mr. Nader or his network of groups are supplied in this appendix.

Accountants for the Public Interest, Inc.

Address:	45 John Street, Rm. 808, New York, NY 10038.
Incorporated:	1974 in California.
Tax Status:	Exempt under IRC Section 501 (c) (3).
Purpose:	"API was founded . . . by accountants concerned with helping minority and consumer organizations deal with complicated fiscal problems relating to health, housing, environmental, and educational issues, and other matters crucial to their interests."[1]
Activities:	API attempts to provide independent analysis to the public on accounting dimensions of current issues, and provides technical assistance to needy organizations on a volunteer basis. Its affiliates branches throughout the

country provide analysis on cases concerning utility rates, wage disputes, rent increases, tax legislation and mental health care.

API currently operates branches in 21 cities. Vern Rossman serves as executive director.

Black Affairs Council, Inc.
Address: Philadelphia, Pennsylvania.
Note: No current information about the Black Affairs Council is available. It received a grant of $1,000 from the Center for Study of Responsive Law in 1972. Its phone number is no longer listed with Philadelphia directory assistance and has apparently become inactive.

California Citizen Action Group
Note: The California Citizen Action Group was formed in the early 1970s with the assistance of Public Citizen's Citizen Action Group.[2] There is no answer at its listed telephone number, however, and no current information about California PIRG is available. The organization may be either inactive or defunct.

Capitol Hill News Service, Inc.
Address: Washington, D.C.
Incorporated: 12/24/74 in D.C.
Dissolved: 5/8/78
Tax Status: Was exempt under IRC Section 501 (c) (3).
Purpose: "Educating and informing the public

Activities: regarding the activities of members of Congress, the operation of the congressional legislative process and the functioning of the news media."[3]

Activities: The News Service provided small-town newspapers, which did not have Washington correspondents, with consumer-oriented news about the activities of their local congressmen.[4] It was intended to supplement the congressmen's own press releases.

The Service was funded by Public Citizen, Inc.

Center for Auto Safety, Inc.
Address: 1346 Connecticut Ave., N.W., 1223, Washington, D.C. 20036.
Incorporated: June 11, 1970, in D.C.
Tax Status: Exempt under IRC Section 501 (c) (3).
Purpose: "To decrease human and economic losses resulting from lack of adequate vechicle [sic] safety,"[5]
Activities: "It monitors complaints and works through the U.S. Department of Transportation for better motor vehicle safety standards."[6]

Mr. Nader was reportedly instrumental in founding the Center, although he is not listed as an incorporator.[7] An ex-employee of Public Citizen and personal friend of Mr. Nader, Clarence Ditlow III, serves as the Center's current director.[8]

The Center has a nationwide membership of several thousand and a staff of 15.

Center for Concerned Engineering
Address: 1346 Connecticut Ave., N.W., 1223, Washington, D.C. 20036.

Founded: Approximately 1971 in Washington, D.C.

Tax Status: The Center for Concerned Engineering is not listed in Internal Revenue Service records as tax-exempt.[9]

Purpose: "Non-membership engineering association which investigates the design history of products with particularly high or unnecessary injury rates; promotes research and development of products which are vitally needed but not necessarily profitable to manufacturers; advocates inventors' rights."[10]

Activities: "Develops new designs for wheelchairs and other technological devices used by disabled persons. The Center provides technical services for, among others, the Veterans Administration, the National Center for Barrier Free Environments, the National Science Foundation, Oberlin College, and the American Academy for the Advancement of Science."[11]

We were unable to reach the Center's Director, Ralf Hotchkiss, for further information.

Center on Corporate Responsibility, Inc. (formerly, Project on Corporate Responsibility, Inc.)

Address: (Of registered agent) U.S. Corporation company, National Press Building, 529 14th St., N.W., Washington, D.C. 20004.

Incorporated: 2/2/70 in D.C. as the "Project on Corporate Responsibility, Inc." Name amended to "Center on Corporate Responsibility, Inc." on 8/14/72.

Tax Status: Exempt under IRC Section 501 (c) (3).

Purpose: "To generate managerial awareness of the compatability of corporate and social interests, and to promote corporate responsiveness to social needs and problems including, but without limitation to, minority group problems and employment discrimination, pollution and utilization and conservation of natural resources and otherwise."[12]

Activities: "At the General Motors Stockholders' meeting in Detroit on May 21 [1970], the Project on Corporate Responsibility offered a proposal to establish a Shareholders' Committee for Corporate Responsibility to report on the company's efforts to produce cars that are safer, nonpolluting, and cheaper to repair. Their chief effort was directed toward the election of three new directors to represent the public interest."[13]

The Project received only 2.73 percent of the vote supporting the Shareholders' Committee and even less for their proposed directors. Although they tried again the following year, they received an even smaller percentage of the vote.[14]

The Project on Corporate Responsibility, also known as "Campaign GM," was initiated in 1970 by two lawyers, Geoffrey Cowan and Phillip W. Moore, III. Its initiation was announced on February 7, 1970, at a press conference held by Messrs. Cowan and Moore with Mr. Nader. The aim of the Project was "to open the management of large corporations to public scrutiny and public influence."[15]

In 1972, the Project amended its name to "Center

on Corporate Responsibility." Currently, the Center "engages in and conducts educational and charitable activities on a non-profit basis for the improvement and betterment of conditions of American life and institutions."[16]

Center for Science in the Public Interest

Address:	1755 S Street, N.W., Washington, D.C. 20009.
Incorporated:	2/25/71 in D.C.
Tax Status:	Exempt under IRS Section 501 (c) (3).
Purpose:	"A. To conduct research and educational programs regarding the effects of science and technology on society and especially on the poor.
	"B. To encourage scientists and engineers through published materials and other means to be socially responsible when their research impinges on vital public interests."[17]
Activities:	"Watchdogs federal agencies that oversee food safety, trade and nutrition. Conducts investigations, and then follows up by publicizing the problems and initiating legal actions designed to improve governmental and corporate policies . . . . Recent actions included encouraging better food labeling and working against deceptive food advertising. . . ." Has published *Nutrition Action* magazine monthly since 1974.[18]

In February 1981, the Center compiled a petition complaining of the "hidden" sodium content in many foods. It planned to present the petition to Health and Human Services Secretary Schweiker.

CSPI has 20,000 members nationwide and a staff of 16.[19]

The incorporators and initial directors of CSPI were former employees of Mr. Nader's Center for the Study of Responsive Law.[20] Three of them still serve on CSPI's Board of Directors: Michael F. Jacobson, Kenneth Lasson, and James Sullivan. Mr. Sullivan serves as CSPI's current president.

Center for Women Policy Studies

Address: 2000 P Street, N.W., 508, Washington, D.C. 20036.

Incorporated: 3/3/72 in D.C.

Tax Status: Exempt under IRC Section 501 (c) (3).

Purpose: "Policy studies and policy review on legal and economic issues affecting women."[21]

Activities: The Center is currently engaged in two projects concerning domestic violence, one in cooperation with the Law Enforcement Administration and the other with the U.S. Department of Health and Human Services. The Center conducts research, maintains a library, and issues a monthly newsletter, but engages in no lobbying.[22]

When the Center was incorporated in 1972 in Washington, Public Citizen provided the seed money and original office space for the Center.[23] Jane Chapman serves as the Center's executive director.

Citizen Action Fund

Address: The Fund's address is listed with D.C. Directory Assistance as 325 Pennsylvania Ave., S.E. That address is, how-

	ever, currently occupied by the "Business Exchange."
Incorporated:	2/6/76 in D.C.
Tax Status:	Exempt under IRC Section 501 (c) (4).
Purpose:	"To raise funds for independent groups working to assure citizens a voice in the formation of public policy and to engage in research and writing and provide the results of such research and other facts and information to Members of Congress and the executive branch of Government of the United States on important public issues concerning the social welfare. . . ."[24]
Activities:	The Fund's Articles of Incorporation state that it may engage in activities as "are consistent with the objectives of Public Citizen, Consumer Action Now; Environmental Action, Environmental Policy Center and Consumer Federation of America."[25]
Note:	No information about the current activities of the Citizen Action Fund is available, as its present address and phone number are not listed. It may, therefore, be presently inactive or defunct.

Citizen Action Group

Address:	CAG is still listed in the Building Directory at 1346 Connecticut Ave., N.W., Washington, D.C. 20036.
Founded:	Approximately 1971, in Washington, D.C.

Tax Status: CAG is not listed in IRS files as tax-exempt.[26]

Purpose: "Builds, trains and services public interest advocacy groups at the state and community levels. Since 1970 CAG has helped to create student-supported Public Interest Research Groups in twenty-one states and citizen-funded Citizen Action Groups in Connecticut and California."[27]

Note: CAG is presently inactive, according to Mr. Mike Horrocks, Director of Public Citizen's Visitors Center.[28] It is not, however, defunct, according to Emmy Smith, accountant for Public Citizen and the Center for the Study of Responsive Law.[29]

Clean Water Action Project, Inc.

Address: 1341 G Street, N.W., Washington, D.C. 20005.

Incorporated: 9/1/71 in D.C. as "Fishermen's Clean Water Action Project, Inc." Name amended to its present form on 1/6/76.

Tax Status: Exempt under IRC Section 501 (c) (4).

Purpose: "The CWAP works for water pollution control and safe drinking water through research, lobbying, education, and advocacy."[30]

Activities: Goals of CWAP include "the elimination of water pollution, the safeguarding of drinking water, and the preservation and protection of water resources." They have focused their lobbying and advocacy efforts on the U.S.

Congress in the past, but are now becoming more interested in promoting
"grass-roots" activity.[31]

The Project was incorporated on September 1,
1971, in Washington, D.C. as the "Fishermen's Clean
Water Action Project." It began as a Nader "task
force."[32] David Zwick serves as president of CWAP.

Clearinghouse for Professional Responsibility, Inc.

Address: Washington, D.C.

Incorporated: 12/17/71 in D.C.

Purpose: "To encourage and aid professionals
                 and other employed citizens to report
                 decisions, activities and products that
                 threaten human safety and health or
                 that threaten to financially disadvan-
                 tage other citizens to responsible per-
                 sons within their organizations, and
                 failing that, to other responsible indi-
                 viduals and organizations."[33]

Activities: "Promoted and encourage [sic] profes-
                 sional responsibility through publicity,
                 articles, speeches, contacts with pro-
                 fessional groups and individual pro-
                 fessionals; sought legal assistance in
                 response to inquiries."[34]

Note: The Clearinghouse was reportedly de-
                 funct by 1973.[35]

The Clearinghouse was incorporated on December 17, 1971, in Washington, D.C. Mr. Nader was one of
its initial directors. Since the Clearinghouse has not
filed an annual report (as required by law) with the D.C.
Corporate Records Office since 1973, we presume it is
now defunct or at least currently inactive.

Commission for the Advancement of Public Interest Organizations

Address: 1875 Connecticut Ave., N.W. Washington, D.C. 20009.

Founded: 1974 in D.C.

Tax Status: The Commission is not listed in IRS files as tax-exempt.[36]

Purpose: "To expand the constituency and capabilities of the public interest movement through the collection and dissemination of information."[37]

Activities: CAPIO seeks to "expand the constituency and capabilities of the public interest movement" without concentrating on any "particular issue."[38] They collect information and publish a guide to "Periodicals of Public Interest Organizations."[39]

   CAPIO is controlled by three commissioners who "set policy and general guidelines."[40] They are Claire Nader (sister of Mr. Ralph Nader), Samuel Epstein and William Monsour. As of June 26, 1980, CAPIO had no acting director.[41] CAPIO has a staff of varying size.

Congress Probe

Address: Congress Probe is still listed in the Building Directory at 1346 Connecticut Ave., N.W., Washington, D.C. 20036. It was sharing Suite 415 with the Public Interest Research Group.

Note: Congress Probe published a weekly newsletter of the same name about events in Congress. Its last issue was published in June 1980.[42] Congress Probe is now defunct.

Congress Project

Address: Washington, D.C.

Founded: November 1971 in D.C.

Purpose: The Project's purpose was "to concentrate on dynamic and internal forces [in the U.S. Congress], to diagnose deficiencies, record strengths and recommend the ways and means of effecting the desired changes based on past experience of the Congress and future prospects for reforms."[43]

Note: The Congress Project has completed its study and is no longer active.

The Congress Project was initiated in November 1971 in Washington, D.C.

Between 1972 and 1975, the Congress Project published individual profiles of members of Congress six reports about specific aspects of Congress, and a book entitled *Who Runs Congress?*

Connecticut Citizen Action Group

Address: 130 Washington Street, Hartford, CT 06106.

Incorporated: 10/15/71 in Connecticut.

Tax Status: Exempt under IRC Section 501 (c) (4).

Purpose: "To promote the common good and general welfare of the people of the United States by combating environmental deterioration, by urging and aiding the establishment of teams of professional advocates; to promote social welfare by encouraging responsible conduct by corporations and government toward man and his environment."[44]

Activities: We know nothing about the current activities of CCAG, because its executive director, Miles Rapoport, never returned our call.[45]

Connecticut Citizen Research Group

Address: 130 Washington Street, Hartford, CT 16106.

Incorporated: 9/5/72 in Connecticut.

Tax Status: Exempt under IRC Section 501 (c) (3).

Purpose: "To educate, counsel, and render assistance in the resolution of environmental and consumer matters of a technical nature; to establish an educational clearinghouse on technical matters relating to environmental and consumer protection, to inform Connecticut residents of the problems associated with the protection of the environment and product safety."[46]

Activities: Unavailable; CCRG's director would not speak with us.[47]

CCRG shares a common address and telephone number with the Connecticut Citizen Action Group. Its executive director is also Miles Rapoport.

Consumer Complaint Research Center

Founded: In 1973, as a three-year study.

Purpose: "To analyze these letters [written by citizens to the Center for Study of Responsive Law] and others written to Congressmen, national consumer groups, regulatory agencies, and federal and state consumer affairs offices . . . the operation of grievance handling mechanisms, both public and private, [was] studied, and recommendations [were] made for better procedures and for new institutions and techniques to deal with consumer complaints."[48]

The Center was funded by the Carnegie Corporation through the Center for the Study of Responsive Law.[49] Its Advisory Board was chaired by Mr. Nader's sister, Laura Nader Milleron.

Consumer Federation of America

Address: 1012 14th Street, N.W., Rm. 901, Washington, D.C. 20005.

Incorporated: 10/3/67 in New York.

Tax Status: Exempt under IRC Section 501 (c) (4).

Purpose: "To promote the rights of all consumers, in harmony with the general welfare, through city, county, regional, state, and national groups . . . . To act as a clearinghouse for the exchange of information, ideas and experiences among members. . . ."[50]

Activities: CFA "advances pro-consumer policy before Congress, the Administration, regulatory agencies, and the courts; assists state and local groups; increases public and media awareness of consumer needs. . . . CFA has pushed for strong, sensible and equitable measures which stabilize the economy by assuring that the marketplace includes:
1) competition,
2) protection against fraud and abuse,
3) effective deregulation (but *only* in

those sectors when meaningful competition exists.)"[51]

The Consumer Federation of America was granted a Certificate of Authority to conduct its affairs in Washington, D.C. on June 7, 1976. Its membership is composed of over 200 organizations, which fund the Federation.

Sharon Stark serves as president of CFA's Board. Stephen Brobeck is executive director. The Federation has a staff of "seven or eight."[52]

Consumers Opposed to Inflation in the Necessities (COIN)

Address:	20036 P Street, N.W., 515, Washington, D.C.
Formed:	October 1978 in D.C.
Tax Status:	COIN is not listed in IRS files as tax-exempt.[53]
Purpose:	"To fight inflation in the four basic necessities—health care, food, housing and energy."[54]
Activities:	According to COIN Director Roger Hickey, "Our group's goal is to go after the real causes of inflation, which are the result of industry structures and bad government policy in energy, food, housing and health."[55]

COIN consists of a coalition of some 70 organizations, including Public Citizen and the Consumer Federation of America.

Consumers Union of the U.S., Inc.

Address:	256 Washington Street, Mt. Vernon, NY 10500. Washington Office: 1511 K Street, N.W.
Incorporated:	2/6/36 in New York.

Tax Status: Unavailable.

Purpose: "The purposes of Consumers Union are to provide consumers with information and counsel on consumer goods and services, to give information on all matters relating to the expenditure of the family income, and to initiate and to cooperate with individual and group efforts seeking to create and maintain decent living standards."[56]

Activities: "CU provides information, education and counsel about consumer goods and services and about management of family income. Publishes *Consumer Reports* magazine, films and other educational materials."[57]

Mr. Nader served on Consumers Union's Board of Directors from the end of 1967 to the Fall of 1975.[58]

Council for Public Interest Law

Address: 25 E Street, N.W., Washington, D.C. 20036.

Mailing
Address: 600 New Jersey Ave., N.W., Washington, D.C. 20001.

Incorporated: 8/7/74 in D.C. as "Council for Advancement of Public Interest Law." Name amended to its present form on 10/10/75.[59]

Tax Status: The Council is listed in IRS files as tax-exempt.

Purpose: "To develop a stable and augmented financial base [for public interest law], to secure greater access to the courts, agencies and Congress, and foster the development of institutions to provide additional public interest legal activities."[60]

Activities:
"Recently, the Council has devoted most of its energies to addressing the problem of funding of public interest law. The Council has filed numerous briefs in actions in which attorney's fees awards to public interest attorneys have been challenged by opposing parties. It is also working to encourage more government agencies to establish public participation funding programs for public interest centers or their clients for participation in agency matters or proceedings. . . . Additionally, the Council continues to serve as a resource and information clearinghouse on public interest law practices."[61]

The Council was incorporated on August 7, 1974, in Washington, D.C., as the "Council for Advancement of Public Interest Law." The name was amended to its present form on October 10, 1975. The Council was organized by "a coalition of public interest lawyers, leaders of the organized bar, and private foundations which had a long-standing concern with public interest law."[62]

The Council qualifies as tax-exempt under Section 501 (c) (3) of the Internal Revenue Code of 1954. Nan Aron serves as executive director, with a staff of two persons.

Note: In February 1981 the Council for Public Interest Law was replaced by the Alliance for Justice. The Alliance is a coalition of at least 17 "public interest" and civil rights groups including National Organization of Women, Natural Resources Defense Council, Consumers Union, and Center for Law in the Public Interest. The Alliance was formed to develop strategies that would enable these groups to supplement their revenues with legal fees *paid by the government*. Nan Aron remains executive director of the new Alliance.

Disability Rights Center

Address: 1346 Connecticut Ave., N.W., 1124, Washington, D.C. 20036.

Founded: 1976 in D.C.

Tax Status: Exempt under IRC Section 501 (c) (3).

Purpose: "Advocacy of disability rights, particularly in the area of equal employment in the Federal Government."[63]

Activities: "Engaged in monitoring the enforcement of civil rights legislation affecting disabled people. Disseminates information about civil rights legislation and represents the concerns of the disabled before federal regulatory agencies. . . . Priorities include accessible mass transportation for the disabled and the elderly, federal employment discrimination and the enforcement of the civil rights section of the Rehabilitation Act."[64]

The Disability Rights Center was founded "with the help of Mr. Nader."[65] Co-directors of the Center are Evan Kemp and Vincent Macaluso. It has a staff of three, and a mailing list of 2,000 names.[66]

District of Columbia D.E.S. (Diethylstilbestrol)

Address: 5426 27th Street, N.W. Washington, D.C.

Incorporated: 1978 in D.C.

Tax Status: Application for exemption pending.

Purpose: To work on issues of concern to persons exposed to D.E.S.—which had been used to treat menopausal symptoms.

Activities: Publish a quarterly to inform public of developments in litigation, and reform and medical research on D.E.S. exposure. Testify before the FDA in an attempt to influence legislation without engaging in formal lobbying.[67]

Note: The original D.E.S. organization founded with seed money from the Center for Study of Responsive Law in 1978 has since split into two groups: "D.E.S. Action" and "D.E.S. Registry." This information concerns the D.E.S. Registry only, because we were unable to reach D.E.S. Action for comment.[68]

For the People

Address: Huntington Woods, Michigan.

Note: For the People received a $2,000 grant from Public Citizen in 1974. It has since apparently become defunct; no telephone number or address is available from directory assistance.

Fund for Constitutional Government

Address: 201 Constitution Ave., N.E. Washington, D.C. 20002.

Incorporated: 2/2/74 in D.C. as "Center for Constitutional Government." Name amended to its present form on 3/26/75.

Tax Status: Exempt under IRC Section 501 (c) (3).

Purpose: "Charitable and educational purposes, including for such purposes the fostering of constitutional responsibility in the conduct of the government of the United States of America and the return by government to the principles set forth by the Framers of the Constitution of the United States and the amendments to the Constitution.[69]

Activities: The Fund "litigates against corruption in corporations or government."[70] The Fund has sponsored a variety of programs, including an "Honest Government Project," a "Military Audit Project," a "Project on Open Government," and a "Property Rights Project."[71]

Anne Zille serves as president of the Fund.

Fund for Investigative Journalism, Inc.

Address: 1346 Connecticut Ave., N.W., 1021, Washington, D.C. 20036.

Incorporated: 6/23/69 in D.C.

Tax Status: Unknown.

Purpose: "Its goal will be to advance the common welfare by seeking to assure ethical and legal conduct in all aspects of national life through the production of articles designed to reveal malfunctions in public or private endeavor."[72]

Activities: "The Fund makes grants to writers to enable them to probe abuses of authority or the malfunctioning of institutions and systems which harm the public. . . . The subjects of Fund grants have covered a broad spectrum including environmental hazards, political corruption, invasions of privacy, organized crime, threats to civil rights, and abuses of corporate and union authority."[73]

Executive director of the Fund is Howard Bray. Nick Kotz serves as chairman of the board.

(National) Gray Panthers

Address:	(National Office) 3635 Chestnut Street, Philadelphia, PA 19104.
Founded:	1970 as an association. Incorporated in January, 1977, in Pennsylvania.[74]
Tax Status:	Exempt under IRC Section 501 (c) (4).
Purpose:	"Coalition of young and old people fighting age discrimination in employment, health care, etc."[75]
Activities:	"Lobbies, advocates in court, and organizes around issues involving health care, nursing homes, age discrimination, mandatory retirement, transportation, Social Security, pensions, hearing aids and housing."[76]
Note:	This part of Gray Panthers is now inactive; all work is being done under the Gray Panthers Project Fund.[77]

Gray Panthers has 106 local chapters nationwide, with a total of 40,000 or 50,000 supporters. Its Washington, D.C., branch was incorporated on June 3, 1974. The Retired Professional Action Group of Washington merged with the Gray Panthers in December 1973.

The executive director of National Gray Panthers is Edith Giese. Its national coordinator is Jonathan

Glassman. The national office in Philadelphia, Pennsylvania has a staff of six paid employees.

Gray Panthers Project Fund

Address:	3635 Chestnut Street, Philadelphia, PA 19104.
Founded:	1970. Incorporated 1974 in PA.
Tax Status:	Exempt under IRC Section 501 (c) (3).
Purpose:	"Promoting social welfare through direct assistance or funding of charitable enterprises, education or scientific research directed to study of problems of ageism, break down barriers of isolation between aged and other members of society, investigate social situations and physical conditions affecting aged persons."[78]
Activities:	The Project Fund is currently engaged in class action suits, advocacy, and public education in support of "a national health service, home health care using displaced homemakers, intergenerational housing arrangements, and an end to condominium-development."[79]

The Project Fund was founded in 1970, but not incorporated until 1974 in Pennsylvania. The staff and officers of the Gray Panthers Project Fund are identical to that of National Gray Panthers.[80]

The Legal Services Reporter

Address:	Washington, D.C.
Note:	The Reporter received a grant of $2,500 from Public Citizen in 1973. No current information is available about it, for it

has apparently become defunct.

Maryland PIRG

Address:	(Main branch) 3110 The Main Dining Hall, The University of Maryland, College Park, MD 20742.
Formed:	1972 in Maryland.
Tax Status:	"Non-profit," no more specific information available.[81]
Purpose:	"To do public interest research in the state of Maryland; to train students to play a more active role as citizens; to maintain some form of initiatory democracy."[82]
Activities:	Recent projects have included work on landlord-tenant issues, publication of a Maryland tenant handbook, and work on "consumer protection issues" such as banking services and redlining. Maryland PIRG also engages in lobbying.[83]

Maryland PIRG's main branch is on the campus of the University of Maryland at College Park. Steven Arisumi is executive director.

Monsour Medical Foundation

Address:	60 Lincoln Way, Jeannette, Pennsylvania. Washington Office: 1875 Connecticut Ave., N.W.
Incorporated:	7/12/66 in Westmoreland Co., PA.
Tax Status:	Exempt under IRC Section 501 (c) (3).
Purpose:	"1) To grant scholarships to qualified students in Medical or Nursing Schools;

	2) To grant scholarships to qualified students who are accepted by Medical or Nursing Schools; 3) To purchase or donate needed equipment for health facilities; 4) To construct, lease and/or operate or purchase health facilities and do this on a non-profit basis."[84]
Activities:	Information about the Foundation's current activities was unavailable because no one would return our repeated phone calls.[85]

The Foundation was granted a "Certificate of Authority to conduct its affairs in the District of Columbia" on May 17, 1974. It lists its purposes in D.C. as "leasing and operating an office for the collection, storage and dissemination of medical health, and related technological data."[86]

According to the annual report filed by Monsour Medical Foundation with the D.C. Corporate Records Office on September 2, 1976, Robert G. Nossen serves as president of the Foundation. Shafeek Nader, brother of Ralph Nader, is Monsour's Registered Agent in D.C.

The latest annual report on file at the D.C. Corporate Records Office is for 1976. More recent information is not available. Monsour Medical Foundation representatives would not return our repeated telephone calls.[87]

National Public Interest Research Group Clearinghouse

Address:	5 Beekman Street, 922, New York, NY 10038.
Incorporated:	Originally in D.C. in 1974. Reincorporated in N.Y. in Spring, 1980.
Tax Status:	Exempt under IRC Section 501 (c) (3).

Purpose: "National coordinating office for network of approximately 30 state PIRGs, which are directed and funded by students—Provides technical assistance and training to local PIRGs in areas of consumer protection, environmental quality and social justice.[88]

Activities: Current operations are limited to the training of volunteers working on energy issues, food co-ops, anti-redlining and tenant organizations under a VISTA grant.[89]

National Resource Center for Consumers of Legal Services

Address: 1302 18th Street, N.W., Washington, D.C. 20036.

Founded: 1973 in Washington, D.C.

Tax Status: Exempt under IRC Section 501 (c) (3).

Purpose: "To improve the way legal services are delivered to the economically disadvantaged."[90]

Activities: "Assists groups working to provide their members with better access to lawyers and assists with group or prepaid plans to offer high quality legal services at the lowest possible cost."[91]

The Center is a non-profit organization working in Washington, D.C. "to improve the way legal services are delivered to the economically disadvantaged."[92] Its president is Elliot Bredhoff. Acting executive director is Joanne Pozzo, who succeeded Sandra DeMent Sterling in October 1979.

New Jersey PIRG (NYPIRG)

Address:	204 West State Street, Trenton, N.J. 08608.
Incorporated:	1972 in New Jersey.
Tax Status:	Exempt under IRC Section 501 (c) (4).
Purpose:	NJPIRG is "a social change organization with a two-fold purpose: 1) To allow students to work on real-life issues as part of their academic experience. 2) To alleviate many pressing problems in our society."[93]
Activities:	NJPIRG's activities include lobbying, research, and dissemination of information on issues such as nuclear power, water quality, truth in testing, and women's rights.

New York PIRG (NYPIRG)

Address:	5 Beekman Street, New York, New York 10038.
Founded:	1973.
Tax Status:	Exempt under IRC Section 501 (c) (4).
Purpose:	To identify and evaluate issues involving public policy decisions, publish the research therefore, make recommendations for public action; have representation before governmental agencies; institute law reform through legislative and legal action, where necessary.
Activities:	NYPIRG's activities include lobbying, research and dissemination of information on a variety of consumer, environmental, energy, tax, health, senior citizen and other public policies.

NYPIRG was formed in 1973 according to a model designed by Ralph Nader.[94] Since then it has expanded to 22 offices and more than 100 staff. Donald Ross is executive director of NYPIRG.

Over the years NYPIRG has engaged in extensive efforts to influence several pieces of legislation. The organization has also filed suit on numerous occasions and intervenes regularly in various agency proceedings. NYPIRG also publishes numerous reports and consumer guides including: "A Guide to New York City Public Records"; "A Study of Albany Property Taxes"; and studies of bank abuses in the Bronx, Buffalo and Brooklyn.

Finally, NYPIRG conducts demonstrations and conferences and engages in extensive door-to-door solicitation from the public. These solicitation efforts reach an estimated 1,000,000 people annually.[95]

Ohio Public Interest Action Group, Inc. (OPIAG)

Note: OPIAG was founded in the early 1970s. "During its first year OPIAG was directed by Ralph Nader and members of the Washington, D.C. PIRG."[96]

OPIAG received a grant from Public Citizen in 1973. It has since closed out its file with the Ohio Charitable Foundations Section, so it is presumably defunct. No further information about OPIAG was available.

Pension Rights Center

Address: 1346 Connecticut Ave., N.W., 1019, Washington, D.C. 20036.

Incorporated: 5/6/76 in D.C.

Tax Status: Exempt under IRC Section 501 (c) (3).

Purpose: "To educate and instruct the public

through educational programs and dissemination of information on rights and interests of participants and beneficiaries under the Employees Retirement Income Security Act of 1974."[97]

Activities: The Center "works for the reform of the nation's retirement income programs." It occasionally publishes a small brochure, *Pension Facts.*[98]

The Pension Rights Center was incorporated on May 6, 1976, in Washington, D.C. It qualifies as tax-exempt within the meaning of Section 501 (c) (3) of the Internal Revenue Code of 1954. Ms. Karen Ferguson serves as the Center's Director.

The Press Information Center
Address: Washington, D.C.
Note: The Center was reportedly established by Mr. Nader and the National Press Club in the early 1970s to file suits on behalf of journalists under the Freedom of Information Act.[99] No further information about the Center is available from Public Citizen or the National Press Club.[100] It is apparently now defunct.

Professional Drivers Council for Safety and Health
Address: 2000 P Street, N.W., Washington, D.C. 20036.
Founded: Approximately 1972 in Washington, D.C.
Tax Status: The Council is not listed in IRS files as tax-exempt.[101]

Purpose: To work "for the unionization of truck drivers."[102]

Note: The Council "used to operate out of the Center for Auto Safety" as "a satellite group."[103] It was reportedly established with a grant from Public Citizen in 1972.[104] No further information about the Council is available, because its director refused to speak with us.[105]

Professionals for Auto Safety, Inc.

Address: Washington, D.C.

Incorporated: 8/26/70 in D.C.

Tax Status: Exempt under IRC Section 501 (c) (4).

Purpose: "To support, conduct, encourage, finance, administer and generally promote investigation, study, analysis, research, evaluation, re-evaluation and understanding leading to solution of the problems of motor vehicle safety and of related problems including but not limited to, a reduction of the annual toll of deaths, injuries and other losses on the highways, the need for vehicles which will provide occupants with a protective rather than a hostile environment in the event of a crash."[106]

Activities: Activities included research studies; investigations, disseminations of information and non-partisan study of legislation proposed in Congress and regulations pending before agencies.[107]

Professionals for Auto Safety was incorporated

on August 26, 1970, in Washington, D.C. It was a "spin-off" from the Center for Auto Safety and was intended as a lobbying branch.[108] As of 1971, the group had no formal membership, but a mailing list of 200 professionals.[109]

Note:　　　　　There is no listing of Professionals for Auto Safety with the D.C. area directory assistance, and no information is available from other sources. The group is, therefore, apparently defunct.

Public Equity Corporation
Address:　　　　Larchmont, N.Y.
Incorporated:　 7/8/74 in Delaware.
Tax Status:　　 Unknown.
Purpose:　　　　"Public Equity Corporation . . . is high risk enterprise that exists primarily for the purpose of increasing the access of ordinary citizens to the legal judicial-process. . . . In summary, the Corporation believes that it will be operating fully in the public interest and under the 'equal justice under law' concept as it was traditionally meant to be."[110]
Activities:　　 "Proposed activities included a "Prepaid Legal Services Program," class action litigation, research, and "acting as a center for the collection and publication of information useful to attorneys and other persons interested in consumer litigation."[111]

The Public Equity Corporation was incorporated on July 8, 1974, under the laws of Delaware, although its address was in Larchmont, New York.

Residential Utility Citizen Action Group

RUCAG was initiated by Mr. Nader in 1977 in Washington, D.C.[112] It sought to protect "consumer interests" in residential utility issues. RUCAG became defunct in 1979, and has been succeeded by the similar Citizens Utility Board project of the Center for Study of Responsive Law.

Retired Professional Action Group

The Retired Professional Action Group was founded in 1972 in Washington, D.C. It was started with seed money from Public Citizen.[113] Mr. Nader was one of its initial directors.

RPAG was concerned with the special problems of older people. In December 1973, it merged with National Gray Panthers in Philadelphia, a group with similar concerns. The Retired Professional Action Group, therefore, no longer exists as such.

Rosewater Foundation

Address:	3900 N. Upland Street, Arlington, VA 22207.
Founded:	1/10/63 in N.Y. as a trust entitled "The Robert C. Townsend Foundation." The name was later amended to its present form.
Tax Status:	Exempt under IRC Section 501 (c) (3).
Purpose:	"To devote and apply the property vested by this Agreement in the Trustees and the income to be derived therefrom, exclusively for religious, charitable, scientific, literary, or educational purposes, either directly or by contributions to organizations duly authorized to carry on religious, charita-

ble, scientific, literary, or educational activities. . . ."[114]

Activities: The Foundation's only project at present is making "selective grants" to fund class action suits. This project is funded by the Stern Foundation.[115]

The Rosewater Foundation was founded on January 10, 1963, as a trust in New York. The original name, "The Robert C. Townsend Foundation," was later amended to its present form. The Trust Agreement was made between Robert C. Townsend, Donor, and Robert C. Townsend and Donald A. Petrie, Trustees.

In 1972 the Rosewater Foundation was given to two Nader employees, Mr. Mark Green and Mr. Peter Petkas, along with assets of $80,628.[116] Mr. Harvey Jester, Nader accountant at the time, replaced Mr. Petkas as trustee the following year. Mr. Green and Mr. Jester have remained Rosewater's two trustees.

Southwest Research and Information Center
Address: P.O. Box 4524, Albuquerque, NM 87108.
Incorporated: 1971 in New Mexico.
Tax Status: Exempt under IRC Section 501 (c) (3).
Purpose: "To provide technical, scientific, and legal assistance to community groups and individuals on various environmental and energy issues."[117]
Activities: Issues upon which the Center is currently active include utility rates, mining regulation, and nuclear waste disposal.[118]

The Center conducts "technical and legal research of environmental and energy issues in the Southwest and around the nation."[119] Don Hancock serves as the Center's executive director, and Katherine Montague is president of its board of directors. The Center has a staff of 15.

Transportation Consumer Action Project

Address: 1346 Connecticut Ave., N.W., 715, Washington, D.C. 20036.

Incorporated: 1/4/79 in D.C. as "Consumer Transportation Policy Center. Name amended to its present form on 2/26/79.

Tax Status: Exempt under IRC Section 501 (c) (3).

Purpose: "To promote, encourage and foster increased safety, efficiency, competition, and recognition of consumer and environmental interests in transportation, to conduct research into these issues and inform the public."[120]

Activities: TCAP is currently advocating "consumer issues" such as surface transportation and intercity bus systems.[121]

It has non-voting members including both individuals and "public interest" organizations. Mimi Cutler serves as president of TCAP.

Notes

1. Annual Report of the Carnegie Corporation of N.Y. for the year ending 9/30/79 (Carnegie funded API).

2. Susan Gross, "The Nader Network," *Business and Society Review*, vol. 13, 1975, p. 11.

3. Articles of Incorporation.

4. Statement by Mike Horrocks, Director of Public Citizen's Visitors Center—phone conversation, 8/18/80.

5. Statement of affairs conducted in D.C., filed with D.C. Corporate Records Office, 4/13/79, Annual Report.

6. Ibid.

7. Statement by Faith Little of the Center—phone conversation, 7/2/80.

8. Ibid.

9. Letter dated August 6, 1980, from D. Sadler of IRS's Philadelphia office.

10. *Encyclopedia of Associations*.

11. Information about the Board of Directors compiled by the Disability Rights Center, on whose board Mr. Ralf Hotchkiss (Director of the Center for Concerned Engineering) serves.

12. Articles of Incorporation, as amended on 8/14/72.

13. Charles McCarry, *Citizen Nader* (Saturday Review Press, New York), 1972, pp. 222-23.

14. Ibid., p. 222.

15. Ibid.

16. Statement of affairs conducted in D.C., filed with D.C. Corporate Records Office, 4/9/79 Annual Report.

17. Articles of Incorporation, as amended 11/30/78.

Other Groups Connected with the Network

18. CSPI pamphlet describing 1980 publications.

19. Statement by Tish Brewster, Assistant Director of CSPI—phone conversation, 7/3/80.

20. Constance Holden, "Public Interest: New Group Seeks Redefinition of Scientists' Role," *Science,* vol. 173, 7/9/71.

21. Statement by Jane Chapman, Executive Director of the Center—phone conversation, 6/26/80.

22. Statement by Lejoi Butler of the Center—phone conversation, 8/15/80.

23. Statement by Jane Chapman, Executive Director of the Center—phone conversation, 6/26/80.

24. API pamphlet mailed to Capital Legal Foundation on request, August 1980.

25. Articles of Incorporation.

26. Letter from D. Sadler of IRS's Philadelphia office.

27. Susan Gross, "The Nader Network," p. 11.

28. Interview, 6/5/80.

29. Phone conversation, 6/2/80.

30. Statement of affairs conducted in D.C., filed with D.C. area public outreach program—phone conversation, 6/25/80.

31. Statement by Gary Steinberg, canvas director of CWAP's D.C. area public outreach program—phone conversation, 6/25/80.

32. Ibid.

33. Articles of Incorporation.

34. Statement of Affairs conducted in D.C., filed with D.C. Corporate Records Office, 4/21/73, Annual Report.

35. Statement by Mike Horrocks—phone conversation, 8/18/80.

36. Letter of 8/6/80 from D. Sadler of IRS.

37. Statement by Karla Jamir, Office Manager—phone conversation, 6/26/80. Confirmed 6/27/80 after Ms. Jamir double-checked her account with officials in her office.

38. Statement by Karla Jamir, Office Manager for CAPIO—phone conversation, 6/26/80.

39. Ibid.

40. Ibid.

41. Ibid.

42. Statement by Marilyn Osterman, Office Manager of PIRG/CARG—phone conversation, 8/14/80.

43. Speech by Ralph Nader to the National Press Club, November 1971. Quoted by Ralph de Toledano in *Hit and Run* (Arlington House Publishers, New Rochelle), 1975, p. 80.

44. Registration statement filed with the State of Connecticut on 5/31/79.

45. Miles Rapoport—never returned our call of 8/14/80.

46. Registration statement filed with the state of Connecticut on 6/1/79.

47. Miles Rapoport—never returned our call of 8/14/80.

48. Annual Report of the Carnegie Corporation of N.Y. for the year ending 9/30/73.

49. Ibid.

50. Articles of Incorporation.

51. CFA pamphlet sent to Capital Legal Foundation upon request.

52. Statement by Ruth Simon, CFA's Information Officer—phone conversation, 8/15/80.

53. Letter of 8/6/80 from D. Sadler of IRS.

54. 1980-81, *Contacts in Consumerism*, ed. Ann Harvey (Fraser/Associates, Washington, D.C.), 1980.

Other Groups Connected with the Network

55. "Business-caused Inflation," *Congressional Quarterly*, 1/20/79, p. 89.

56. "Profile" of Consumers Union issued on 4/1/79 by the Washington, D.C., Foundation for Public Affairs.

57. 1980-81, *Contacts in Consumerism*.

58. Statement by David Berliner, Associate Director of Consumers Union—phone conversation, 6/30/80.

59. Letter of 8/6/80 from D. Sadler of IRS.

60. Literature distributed by the Council at the Public Interest Law Conference which it sponsored January 3 and 4, 1980 in D.C.

61. Literature from the Council, sent to Capital Legal Foundation upon request.

62. Literature from the Council, sent to Capital Legal Foundation upon request and received 8/4/80.

63. Statement by Karen Snyder, Office Manager—phone conversation, 7/2/80.

64. 1980-81, *Contacts in Consumerism*.

65. Statement by Karen Snyder, Office Manager of the Disability Rights Center—phone conversation, 7/3/80.

66. Ibid.

67. Statement by Ms. Phyllis Wetherill of D.E.S. Registry—phone conversation, 8/14/80.

68. On 8/14/80 we called D.E.S. Action and left a message on their phone recorder asking them to return our call. They did not do so. We spoke on the same day to Ms. Phyllis Wetherill of D.E.S. Registry, who gave us the information included here.

69. Articles of Incorporation.

70. Statement by Annie Zill, President of FCG—phone conversation, 7/7/80.

71. "Profile" of the Fund published on 7/1/77 by the Washington, D.C., Foundation for Public Affairs.

72. Articles of Incorporation.

73. FIJ brochure sent to Capital Legal Foundation upon request.

74. Statement by Jean Hooper, Librarian of National Gray Panthers—phone conversation, 6/3/80.

75. Statement by Jean Hooper, librarian from Gray Panthers—phone conversation, 7/2/80.

76. 1980-81, *Contacts in Consumerism.*

77. Statement by Jonathan Glassman, National Coordinator of Gray Panthers—phone conversation, 8/14/80.

78. Statement quoted in report issued 3/17/80 by the National Information Bureau, Inc., of New York.

79. Statement by Jonathan Glassman—phone conversation, 8/14/80.

80. Report issued by the National Information Bureau, Inc., of New York on 3/17/80.

81. Statement by Steven Arisumi, Executive Director of Maryland PIRG—phone conversation, 8/15/80.

82. Ibid.

83. Ibid.

84. Articles of Incorporation.

85. Calls made 7/1/80, 7/2/80, 7/3/80. Messages left with Office Manager Karla Jamir were never answered.

86. Application for Certificate of Authority, filed with D.C. Corporate Records Office, 5/17/74.

87. We called on July 1, 2, and 3, 1980, and spoke with Office Manager, Karla Jamir. Our calls were never returned.

88. Quote from 1980-81, *Contacts in Consumerism.* Confirmed by Robin Ferber, Project Coordinator at National PIRG—phone conversation, 7/7/80.

Other Groups Connected with the Network

89. Ibid.

90. Statement by Bill Bolger to NRCCLS—phone conversation, 7/2/80.

91. 1980-81, *Contacts in Consumerism*, p. 215.

92. Statement by Bill Bolger of NRCCLS—phone conversation, 8/17/80.

93. Statement by Debra Ettinger, NJPIRG Chairperson—phone conversation, 8/14/80.

94. Annual Report filed with the State of New York.

95. Ibid.

96. Ralph Nader and Donald Ross, *Action for a Change* (Grossman, New York), 1971. Rev. ed. 1972, p. 144.

97. Articles of Incorporation.

98. 1980-81, *Contacts in Consumerism*, p. 218.

99. Theodore Jacqueney, "Washington Pressures/Nader network switches focus to legal action, congressional lobbying," *National Journal*, 6/9/73, p. 843.

100. Mike Horrocks, Director of Public Citizen's Visitors Center, stated that he had "never heard of" the Press Information Center (phone conversation, 8/18/80). We were informed by the National Press Club that they had never had any connection with Mr. Nader or a Press Information Center (phone conversation, 8/14/80).

101. Letter of 8/6/80 from D. Sadler of IRS.

102. Statement by Mike Horrocks—phone conversation, 8/18/80.

103. Ibid.

104. Susan Gross, "The Nader Network," p. 9.

105. Michael Goldberg, Director—phone conversation, 7/3/80.

106. Articles of Incorporation.

107. Ibid.

108. Lois G. Wark "Consumer Report/Nader campaigns for funds to expand activities of his consumer action complex," *National Journal*, 9/8/71, p. 1909.

109. Ibid.

110. Statement filed with the Securities and Exchange Commission, 12/11/74.

111. Ibid.

112. Statement by Mike Horrocks—phone conversation, 8/18/80.

113. Susan Gross, "The Nader Network," *Business and Society Review*, vol. 13, 1975, p. 14.

114. Trust Agreement.

115. Statement by Harvey Jester, a trustee of Rosewater—phone conversation, 7/9/80.

116. Barbara O'Reilley, "Nader Series," written for Gannett News Service, 3/29/79.

117. Statement by Don Hancock, Director of SWRIC—phone conversation, 8/14/80.

118. Ibid.

119. Statement by Don Hancock, Director of SWRIC—phone conversation, 7/9/80.

120. Articles of Incorporation.

121. Statement by Cornish Hitchcock, who identified himself as TCAP's "Legal Advisor"—phone conversation, 7/7/80.

Appendix E
Statute Summaries

Twenty-three states and the District of Columbia have adopted standard solicitation acts. Eighteen states have not adopted any act. The other nine states take differing approaches to the problem. A state-by-state analysis follows:

Alabama—No statute.

Alaska—No statute.

Arizona—No statute.

Arkansas

Applicable Statute: Arkansas Stat. Ann. Section 64-1601 et seq. (1959).

Statute Summary: The statute prohibits solicitation of contributions "by any means whatsoever" by any charitable organization until the organization registers with the Secretary of State. The organization must then file an annual report with the secretary of state within 90 days following the end of its fiscal year. The report must include total amount of funds received and fund-raising costs.

Exemptions: "Charitable Organization" is defined as "any benevolent, philanthropic, patriotic, or eleemosynary person or one purporting to be such." The act does not apply (1) where contributions are solicited solely from persons who are members of the organization; (2) where solicitations are made solely for church, missionary, or religious purposes; and (3) where the organization does not receive contributions in excess of $1,000 (provided that all fund-raising is carried on by persons who are unpaid for their services, and provided that no part of the organization's assets or income inures to the benefit of any officer or member).

Penalties: Any person who conducts a solicitation without filing under the act or who files false information shall be punished by a fine not to exceed $500.00 or by imprisonment for not more than six months, or both.

State Contact Person: Velma Caple, Secretary of State's Office, Little Rock, Arkansas 72201, (501) 370-5166.

Organizations Registered: None.

California

Applicable Statute: California has no charitable solicitation act. However, Cal. Bus. and Prof. Code Section 17510 et seq. (1972) regulates "sales solicitations" by noncharitable organizations.

Statute Summary: Prior to any sales solicitation for charitable purposes, the seller must exhibit a card entitled "Sale for Charitable Purposes Card." The card must give the name and addresses of the soliciting organization, the amount that will be given to the organization, and the amount that will be used for charitable purposes. The card must be signed by an officer of the soliciting organization.

246

Exemptions: Any organization which at the time of the sales solicitation for charitable purposes has charitable tax-exempt status under federal and state laws is not subject to the act.

Penalties: Violation may result in a fine, imprisonment, or both.

State Contact Person: Larry W. Campbell, Registrar of Charitable Trusts, Department of Justice, P.O. Box 13447, Sacramento, CA 95813, (916) 445-2021.

Organizations Registered: Public Citizen, Inc.

Colorado

Applicable Statute: No charitable solicitation statute. However, Colorado Criminal Code Section 18-5-115 (1975) prohibits "charitable fraud."

Statute Summary: Charitable fraud includes (1) soliciting or receiving a contribution for a purpose which leads the donor to believe that the contribution is not intended to be so used; (2) utilizing the name of another without consent; and (3) soliciting contributions for a charitable purpose and using a name or symbol so similar to that of another organization, that the use is calculated to mislead the donor.

Exemptions: No exemptions.

Penalties: A fine, imprisonment, or both.

State Contact Person: Mr. Stephen Kaplan, Office of the Attorney General, Legal Services Section, 1525 Sherman, Third Floor, Denver, Colorado 80218, (203) 839-3611.

Organizations Registered: No registration required.

Connecticut

Applicable Statute: Conn. Gen. Stat. Section 17-21e et. seq. 1963, as amended in 1976.

Statutory Summary: Every non-exempt charitable organization must register with the Department of Consumer Protection. The registration statement must be refiled in each subsequent year in which the organization solicits funds within the state.

Exemptions: Seventeen types of organizations are exempted from the registration requirement. Included are religious organizations, parent-teacher associations, accredited educational institutions, hospitals, public libraries, and organizations that receive less than $5,000 annually in contributions. Exemption is not automatic. An organization believing itself to be exempt must submit a statement in support of that belief.

Penalties: Violation of the statute can lead to revocation of registration, a fine of not more than $1,000, and/or imprisonment for not more than one year.

State Contact Person: David E. Ormstedt, Assistant Attorney General, Room 177 State Office Building, Hartford, Conn. 06115, (203) 566-3035.

Organizations Registered: None.

Delaware—No statute.

District of Columbia
Applicable Statute: D.C. Code Section 2-2101 et seq. (1957).

Statute Summary: The act requires every person who solicits charitable contributions to hold a certificate of registration, issued by the Department of Economic Development. The certificate must be applied for at least 15 days before solicitation begins. A person may not, for compensation, make a telephone solicitation for charitable purposes in the District of Columbia.

Exemptions: Tax-exempt churches, other religious organizations, and organizations which solicit exclusively among their membership are exempt from the law.

Penalties: Any person violating any provision of the Act, or filing an application containing any false statement, may be punished by a fine of not more than $500, imprisonment of not more than 60 days, or both.

State Contact Person: Mr. Chester McKenzie, Department of Licenses, Investigations, and Inspections, Office of Licenses and Permits, North Potomac Building, 614 H Street, N.W., Washington, D.C. 20001. (202) 727-3666.

Organizations Registered: None.

Florida

Applicable Statute: Florida Stats. Chap. 496 (1974).

Statute Summary: Every non-exempt charitable organization that intends to solicit in-state contributions must register with the Department of State. The registration statement must be refiled each year. All filed information becomes part of the public record.

Three types of organizations are exempted: membership groups, organizations that receive less than $4,000 in annual contributions from more than ten persons and those whose activities are conducted by volunteers. Exemption is not automatic. The organization must submit an application for exempt status—churches and other tax-exempt religious institutions need not register.

Penalties: Violation of the statute can lead to an investigation, revocation of registration, or criminal prosecution.

State Contact Person: Margery Gate, Charitable

Solicitations Coordinator, Department of State, Division of Licensing, The Capital, Tallahassee, Florida 32304, (904) 488-5381.

Organizations Registered: None.

Georgia

Applicable Statute: Georgia Code Ann., Chap. 35-10 (1980). The law requires every charitable organization (unless exempted) which intends to solicit within the state to file a registration statement with the Department of State.

Exemptions: Seven categories of organizations are exempted: religious organizations, educational institutions, business and trade associations, certain civic, fraternal, patriotic and social groups, certain local community organizations, organizations of hunters, fisherman, and target shooters, and organizations that receive less than $15,000 per year. Persons who seek contributions for the relief of a specified individual are also exempt.

Penalties: Violation may result in an investigation, injunctive proceedings, private actions, revocation of registration, or civil or criminal prosecution. In any civil action, if the court finds intential violations, the state may recover a penalty not exceeding twice the amount collected.

State Contact Person: Cicero Lucas, Secretary of State's Office, State Capital, Atlanta, Georgia 30334, (404) 656-2859.

Organizations Registered: None.

Hawaii

Applicable Statute: Hawaii Rev. Stats., Title 23, Chap. 467B (1971).

Statute Summary: Every non-exempt charitable organization must file a registration statement with the director of regulatory agencies. The statement must be refiled in each subsequent year. All documents and information filed become public records.

Exemptions: There are seven exempt categories—religious organizations and agencies, educational institutions, non-profit hospitals, certain organizations that have volunteer fund-raising efforts, membership groups, and organizations that receive less than $4,000 annually in contributions from more than ten persons. Exemption is not automatic. An organization believed exempt must submit an application for the exemption.

Penalties: Violation can lead to an investigation, suspension or revocation of registration, injunctive action, or criminal prosecution.

State Contact Person: Russell Nagata, Corporation and Securities Administrator, Business Registration Division, Department of Regulatory Agencies, 1010 Richards Street, Honolulu, Hawaii 96813, (808) 548-4740.

Organizations Registered: None

Idaho—No statute.

Illinois

Applicable Statute: Ill. Ann. Stats. Section 23-S101 et seq. (1974).

Statute Summary: A registration statement must be filed with the attorney general. The statement remains in effect until cancelled or withdrawn. All filed documents become public records.

Exemptions: There are nine categories that are exempted: accredited educational institutions, libraries, certain federally charted organizations, boys' clubs, certain membership groups, and organizations that receive less than $4,000 in annual contributions and whose fund-raising functions are carried on by volunteers. Churches and other religious organizations are also exempt. These groups must file an initial registration statement and then be notified of exemption by the attorney general.

Penalties: The Illinois attorney general has authority to act against a charitable organization that violates the charitable solicitation act. Violation of registration may invite civil or criminal prosecution.

State Contact Person: Robert Tingler, Chief, Charitable Trusts and Solicitations Division, Office of the Attorney General, 188 West Randolph, Room 1826, Chicago, IL 60601, (312) 792-2595.

Organizations Registered: Public Citizen, Inc.

Indiana—No statute.

Iowa

Applicable Statute: Iowa Code Ann., Vol. 1, Title 5, Ch. 122, Section 122.1 et seq. (1967).

Statute Summary: An organization that intends to solicit contributions in Iowa must either be incorporated under Iowa law or be authorized to do business in the state. The Secretary of State has full discretion in allowing a solicitation. The charitable organization must obtain a permit from the Secretary of State which expires at the end of each calendar year.

Exemptions: Local organizations, churches, and schools are exempt.

Penalties: Violation of the statute can lead to a fine, imprisonment, or both.

State Contact Person: Elizabeth A. Nolan, Assistant Attorney General, State House, Des Moines, Iowa 50319, (515) 281-5164.

Organizations Registered: None.

Kansas

Applicable Statute: Kansas Stats. Ann. Section 17-1739 et seq. (1974).

Statute Summary: Every soliciting organization must either be incorporated under Kansas law or be authorized to do business in Kansas. Before commencing solicitation, an organization must file a registration statement with the secretary of state. If the organization receives more than $10,000 annually in contributions or if its fund-raising is conducted by non-volunteers, it must file a detailed annual report. The attorney general has the authority to enjoin a solicitation where a false statement is made in any application or registration statement.

Exemptions: There are 13 exemption categories, including religious organizations, educational institutions, fraternal and historical societies, volunteer firemen organizations, Boy and Girl Scouts of America, and organizations that receive less than $5,000 in annual contributions.

Penalties: The attorney general may bring an action, on behalf of the state, against any charitable organization in violation of the Act, to enjoin the organization from continuing solicitation, or to cancel any registration statement previously filed.

State Contact Person: Linda Jeffrey, Assistant Attorney General, Kansas Judicial Center, 301 West 10th Street, Topeka, Kansas 66612, (913) 296-2236.

Organizations Registered: None.

Kentucky

Applicable Statute: Kentucky Revised Stats. Sections 196.250 (1974), 367.510-367.650, and 367.670.

Statute Summary: No foreign corporation is authorized to do business in the state until it has filed a certified copy of its articles of incorporation with the secretary of state.

Exemptions: Solicitations by an organization of its bona fide members, solicitations by a religious organization for religious purposes, solicitations by educational student groups or parent-teacher associations are all exempt from the law.

Penalty: Violation of the statute can lead to civil and/or criminal penalties.

State Contact Person: Richard O. Wyatt, Assistant Attorney General, 209 St. Clair Street, Frankfort, Kentucky 40601, (502) 564-6607.

Organizations Registered: None.

Louisiana—No statute.

Maine

Applicable Statute: Maine Rev. Stats. Ann. Section 5001 et seq. (1978).

Statute Summary: A registration statement must be filed with the secretary of state, and refiled in each subsequent year in which the charitable organization solicits contributions in the state. If the organization receives more than $30,000 in gross contributions during the year, it must file an annual report within six months of the close of its fiscal year.

Exemptions: Five types of organizations need not file: membership groups, religious organizations, accredited educational institutions, non-profit hospitals, and organizations that receive less than $10,000 annually, provided that all fund-raising is done by volunteers. Exemption is not automatic; the organization must submit an application for exemption.

Penalties: A violation of the act is a violation of the state's unfair trade practices act and an *intentional* violation is a crime.

State Contact Person: Assistant Attorney General, Consumer and Anti-trust Division, Department of the Attorney General, State Office Bldg., Augusta, Maine 04333, (207) 289-3716.

Organizations Registered: None.

Maryland

Applicable Statute: Ann. Code of Maryland, Art. 41, Section 41-103 et seq. (1976).

Statute Summary: Every non-exempt organization must file a registration statement with the Department of State. The statement must be refiled each year, and if the organization decides to terminate in-state solicitation, it must file a statement to that effect.

Exemptions: Accredited educational institutions, non-profit hospitals and related institutions, membership groups, tax-exempt religious organizations, veterans' organizations, and organizations that receive less than $5,000 in contributions each year as long as fund raising is carried on by volunteers. Exemption is not automatic, however.

Penalties: Violation of the Maryland statute can lead to an investigation, revocation of registration, and/or civil or criminal prosecution. An organization which fails to file a registration statement with the secretary of state, or files a false statement, is guilty of a misdemeanor, and may be fined not more than $5,000 or sentenced to imprisonment for not more than one year.

State Contact Person: Skip Bullen, Secretary of State's Office, State Office, Annapolis, MD 21414, (301) 269-3421.

Organizations Registered: None.

Massachusetts

Applicable Statute: Massachusetts General Laws,

Chap. 12, Section 8 et seq. Chap. 69, Section 18 et seq. (1964).

Statute Summary: Every "public charity" which intends to solicit contributions must register with the Division of Public Charities (a part of the attorney general's department) The registration must be renewed each year.

Exemptions: Religious organizations, tax-exempt educational institutions, parent-teacher associations, non-profit hospitals, public libraries, organizations soliciting only their members, volunteer fire companies, and organizations which receive less than $5,000 yearly are all exempted from the registration requirement.

Penalties: Any person who knowingly violates any provision of the act, or who gives false or incorrect information in filing may be fined not more than one thousand dollars or imprisoned not more than one year or both.

State Contact Person: Catherine Hantzis, Assistant Attorney General, Department of the Attorney General, One Ashburton Place, Boston, Mass. 02108 (617) 727-2235.

Organizations Registered: None.

Michigan

Applicable Statute: Michigan Compiled Laws Ann. Section 400-271 et seq. (1975).

Statute Summary: Every non-exempt organization must file an application for a license with the attorney general. The license must then be renewed each year.

Exemptions: Certified educational institutions, hospitals, organizations that serve children and families, tax-exempt religious organizations, and organizations that annually receive less than $8,000 are among those organizations that are exempted from the licensing requirement.

Penalties: Violation can result in an investigation, injunctive action, suspension or revocation of a license, or criminal prosecution.

State Contact Person: Mr. Patrick Isom, Assistant Attorney General, Law Building, Lansing, Michigan 48913, (517) 373-1152.

Organizations Registered: None.

Minnesota

Applicable Statute: Minnesota Stats. Ann., Chap. 309 (1973, as amended in 1975 and 1978).

Statute Summary: A registration statement must be filed with the Securities Division of the Department of Commerce. All documents and information become public records.

Exemptions: Certain religious membership groups, private foundations, educational institutions, certain fraternal and professional societies, and organizations that receive less than $10,000 in annual contributions (and whose fund raising is done by volunteers), are exempt.

Penalties: Violation can result in an investigation, denial, or revocation of a registration or license, injunctive proceedings, or civil or criminal prosecution.

State Contact Person: Assistant Attorney General, Office of the Attorney General, 515 Transportation Bldg., (612) 296-6438.

Organizations Registered: Public Citizen, Inc.

Mississippi—No statute.

Missouri—No statute.

Montana—No statute.

Nebraska

Applicable Statute: Revised Statutes of Nebraska, Chapter 101, Article 14 (1969).

Statute Summary: An organization must file a copy of its governing instruments with the secretary of state, who then issues a certificate permitting solicitation for the remainder of the calendar year.

Exemptions: None.

Penalties: One who solicits for a charity which is not in compliance with the act is guilty of a misdemeanor.

State Contact Person: Helen Lang, Secretary to Deputy, Secretary of State's Office, Lincoln, Nebraska 68509, (402) 471-2554.

Organizations Registered: None.

Nevada

Applicable Statute: Nevada has no charitable solicitations act. However, Nevada Consolidated Laws Section 86-190 (1943) does require that a "national" charitable organization soliciting in the state file an annual report with the secretary of state.

Statute Summary: Not applicable.

Exemptions: Not applicable.

Penalties: Not applicable.

State Contact Person: Deputy Attorney General, Office of the Attorney General, Capital Complex, Carson City, Nebraska 89710, (702) 885-5203.

Organizations Registered: None.

New Hampshire

Applicable Statute: New Hampshire Rev. Stats. Ann. Section 320:20 et seq. (1966).

Statute Summary: The director of the Division of Welfare has authority to issue certificates enabling organizations to solicit funds. Certified organizations must expend at least 85 percent of total receipts for their charitable purpose.

Exemptions: Organizations that have a permanent place of business in the state are exempted. Solicitations by means of direct mail or the media are not subject to the act.

Penalties: A fine and/or imprisonment are both available sanctions.

State Contact Person: Thomas E. Thompson, Deputy Director of Welfare, Eight London Road, Concord, New Hampshire 03301, (603) 271-3272 or (603) 271-3591.

Organizations Registered: None.

New Jersey

Applicable Statute: New Jersey Stats. Ann. Section 45:17A et seq. (1971).

Statute Summary: A registration statement must be filed with the attorney general. The registration remains in effect until cancelled or withdrawn. An organization that is organized under another state's laws is deemed to appoint the New Jersey secretary of state as its agent for service of process.

Exemptions: The following organizations are exempted from the registration requirement: Certain fraternal, historical and like membership groups, religious organizations, organizations that receive less than $10,000 annually (provided that all fund-raising is done by volunteers), accredited educational institutions, certain libraries, and organizations operating for the care and treatment of invalid and crippled children.

Penalties: Potential sanctions include an investigation, injunctive proceedings, revocation or denial of registration, or civil or criminal prosecution.

State Contact Person: Frank Svenson, Department of Law and Public Safety, Div. of Consumer Affairs, Charities Registration Section, 1100 Raymond Blvd., Newark, New Jersey 07102, (201) 648-4002.

Organizations Registered: Public Citizen Inc.

New Mexico—No statute.

New York

Applicable Statute: McKinney's Consolidated Laws of New York Ann., Art. 7-A of Executive Law, Chap. 669, Section 171 et seq. (1977).

Statute Summary: Every non-exempt organization must file a registration statement with the secretary of state. The statement remains in effect until cancelled or withdrawn. Registration statements and other documents become public records.

Exemptions: Religious agencies and organizations, accredited educational institutions, certain libraries, certain membership groups, organizations that receive less than $10,000 in annual contributions (as long as fund-raising is done by volunteers) and veteran's organizations are all exempted.

Penalties: Investigation, revocation of registration, and/or civil or criminal prosecution are available sanctions.

State Contact Person: Joseph G. Shea, Associate Accountant, Office of Charities Registration, Department of State, Albany, New York 12231.

Organizations Registered: Public Citizen, Inc.

North Carolina

Applicable Statute: North Carolina General Statutes Section 108-75.1 et seq. (1975).

Statute Summary: Every non-exempt organization must be licensed with the Department of Human Resources. The license application must be refiled each year.

Exemptions: Accredited educational institutions, hospitals, veterans' organizations membership groups, organizations that receive less than $2,000 annually or that receive contributions from less than ten persons, and churches and other religious institutions are exempt. The Department also has the authority to grant exemption to a charitable organization that is organized under another state's law where that law is similar to the North Carolina Act and the organization is exempt from registration under such law.

Penalties: Violation of the act can lead to an investigation, revocation of a license, or criminal prosecution.

State Contact Person: Ed Edgerton, Solicitation Licensing Branch, Department of Human Resources, Div. of Facility Svcs., P.O. Box 12200, Raleigh, North Carolina 27605, (919) 733-4510.

Organizations Registered: None.

North Dakota

Applicable Statute: North Dakota Century Code, Title 50, Chapter 22 (1961, as amended 1975).

Statute Summary: The statute requires all non-exempt organizations to obtain licenses from the secretary of state before commencing solicitation. The license is valid for one year.

Exemptions: The law does not apply to religious organizations, organizations soliciting funds for churches operating within the state or for institutions of higher learning, and Boy and Girl Scouts of America groups.

Penalties: Violation of the statute is a misdemeanor under North Dakota law.

State Contact Person: Deputy to the Secretary of State, Bismark, North Dakota 58501.

Organizations Registered: None.

Ohio

Applicable Statute: Page's Ohio Revised Code Ann., Title 17, Chapter 1716 (1955).

Statute Summary: The organization must register with the state attorney general or county clerk of courts. Registration remains effective as long as the information on file remains "complete, accurate, and current."

Exemptions: Educational institutions, membership groups, organizations that receive less than $500 annually, and religious agencies and organizations are exempted from the registration requirements.

Penalties: Violators may be fined up to $500 or imprisoned for six months, or both.

State Contact Person: Richard C. Farrin, Charitable Foundations Section, Office of the Attorney General, Columbus, Ohio 43215.

Organizations Registered: None.

Oklahoma

Applicable Statute: Oklahoma Statutes Ann. Section 18.552-1 (1978).

Statute Summary: Every non-exempt charitable organization must register with the state auditor and inspector. The registration must be renewed in each subsequent year.

Exemptions: Religious organizations, educational institutions, and certain membership groups are exempted.

Penalties: Violation of the statute may result in an

investigation, initiation of an injunctive action, loss of tax exemption, revocation of registration, or criminal prosecution.

State Contact Person: Don McCombs, Jr., Legal Counsel, State Capitol, Room 100, Oklahoma City, Okla. 73105, (405) 521-3495.

Organizations Registered: None.

Oregon

Applicable Statute: Oregon Revised Statutes, Title 13, Chapter 128, Sections 128.805 through 128.990.

Statute Summary: There is no registration requirement per se. However, every non-exempt organization must file a report annually with the attorney general. The attorney general has express authorization to seek an injunction against solicitation where the organization has failed to comply with the law.

Exemptions: Educational institutions, hospitals, historical societies, museums, religious organizations, organizations soliciting funds only from their members, and organizations that receve $250 or less from a solicitation in any twelve-month period are exempted from compliance.

Penalties: Available penalties include criminal prosecution, fines, or injunctive proceedings.

State Contact Person: Virgil D. Mills, Administrator of Charitable Trusts, Charitable Trust Section, 500 Pacific Building, 520 S.W. Yamhill, Portland, Oregon 97204, (503) 229-5278.

Organizations Registered: None.

Pennsylvania

Applicable Statute: Purdon's Pennsylvania Statues Ann., Title 10, Chapter 4, Section 160-1 et seq. (1974).

Statute Summary: A registration statement must be filed with the Department of the Commonwealth, and must be refiled in each subsequent year. Filed documents and statements become a matter of public record. The Commission on Charitable Organizations has the authority to promulgate rules and regulations in the implementation of the act, prescribe the registration and other forms, and hold hearings and make adjudications.

Exemptions: Accredited educational institutions, hospitals, veterans' organizations, public libraries, membership groups, tax-exempt religious organizations, and organizations that receive less than $7,500 annually in contributions or that do not annually receive contributions from more than ten persons need not file the annual registration statement. However, an organization believing itself to be covered by one of the above exemptions must submit an application for the exemption.

Penalties: The Pennsylvania statute is one of the most strictly enforced of all charitable solicitation acts. Investigation, revocation or suspension of registration, or criminal prosecution may result from a violation of the statute.

State Contact Person: Mr. James Maxey III, Commission on Charitable Organizations, Room 301, North Office B, State Capitol, Harrisburg, PA 17120, (717) 783-1720.

Organizations Registered: Public Citizen, Inc.

Rhode Island

Applicable Statute: General Laws of Rhode Island, Chapter 5, Section 5-52-1 et seq. (1976).

Statute Summary: A registration statement must be filed with the Department of Business Regulation, and renewed each subsequent year. All filed documents and other information become public records. An organization will be denied registration if a statement in its application for registration proves to be false, if the organization has engaged in a fraudulent enterprise, or if the activities to be financed will be incompatible with the health or welfare of the citizens of the state.

Exemptions: Accredited educational institutions, religious organizations, hospitals, public libraries, art museums, and organizations that receive less than $3,000 annually in contributions need not file a registration statement. Exemption is not automatic, however. An application for the exemption must be submitted.

Penalties: An investigation, revocation of registration, or criminal prosecution are all potential penalties.

State Contact Person: Thomas Gorrigan, Department of Business Regulations, 100 North Main Street, Providence, RI 02903, (401) 277-2405.

Organizations Registered: None.

South Carolina

Applicable Statute: South Carolina Code, Title 33, Chapter 55 (1972).

Statute Summary: All non-exempt charitable organizations must register with the secretary of state. The registration statement, as well as an annual report, must be refiled each year. All documents and filed information become public records.

Exemptions: Exempt organizations include tax-exempt religious organizations, accredited educational institutions, hospitals, veterans' organizations, membership groups, and organizations that receive less than $2,000 in annual contributions. Exemption is not automatic.

Penalties: An investigation, revocation of registration, or criminal prosecution are all available sanctions. There is also a Commission on Charitable Organizations which holds hearings and makes adjudications, and makes recommendations to the secretary for enforcement of the act.

State Contact Person: Eric Pantsari, Administrator of Public Charities, Div. of Public Charities, Secretary of State, 816 Keenan Building, Columbia, South Carolina 29201, (803) 758-2244.

Organizations Registered: None.

South Dakota

Applicable Statute: South Dakota Compiled Laws Title 37, chapter 27 (1975).

Statute Summary: Every charitable organization must file a registration statement with the Department of Commerce and Consumer Affairs, and refile in each subsequent year in which solicitations are made within the state.

Exemptions: Churches and other tax-exempt religious organizations, educational institutions, cooperative scholarship corporations, and organizations raising less than $5,000 annually are fully exempt. In addition, non-profit hospitals, veterans' organizations, community health care clinics, membership groups, and organizations that receive less than $10,000 in annual contributions are exempt from the registration fee requirement. Exemption status must be applied for, and will be lost if the organization employs a professional solicitor.

Penalties: Violation can lead to an investigation, injunctive action, revocation or registration, or criminal prosecution.

State Contact Person: Jim Roberson, Division of Charitable Solicitation, Secretary of State's Office, Capitol Hill Building, Nashville, TN 37219, (615) 741-2555.

Organizations Registered: None.

Texas—No statute.

Utah

Applicable Statute: Utah has no charitable solicitation act. However, Utah Code Ann. Section 76-10-601 (1973) prohibits the use of a person's name in connection with a charitable solicitation without consent.

Statute Summary: Not applicable.

Exemptions: Not applicable.

Penalties: Not applicable.

Vermont—No statute.

Virginia—No statute.

Applicable Statute: Code of Virginia Section 57.48 et seq. (1975).

Statute Summary: A registration statement must be filed with the administrator of consumer affairs. Information filed by the organization becomes a matter of public record.

Exemptions: Exempted organizations included churches, political parties, campaign committees, labor unions, trade associations, membership groups, accredited educational institutions, and organizations that receive less than $2,000 in annual contributions. Exemption is not automatic.

Penalties: An investigation, injunctive proceedings, adverse publicity in one or more newspapers, or civil or criminal prosecution are all available as potential sanctions.

State Contact Person: Jim Morano, Office of Consumer Affairs, 125 East Broad Street, Richmond, VA 23219, (804) 786-1343.

Organizations Registered: None.

Washington

Applicable Statute: Revised Code of Washington Ann., Title 19, Chapter 9 (1973).

Statute Summary: Charitable organizations, unless exempt, must file an application for registration with the Department of Motor Vehicles. The registration remains in effect unless withdrawn by the organization or revoked by the director. Filed documents become public records.

Exemptions: Religious organizations, certain hospital organizations, government subdivisions, membership groups, radio and television stations, legal newspapers, and organizations that receive less than $10,000 in annual contributions or that do not receive contributions from more than ten persons are exempted from the entirety of the statute.

Penalties: Available penalties include an investigation, revocation of registration, injunctive action, or criminal prosecution.

State Contact Person: Mr. Ray Whalin, Division of Professional Licensing, Charities Section/Dept. of Licensing, Olympia, Washington 98501, (206) 753-1966.

Organizations Registered: None.

West Virginia

Applicable Statute: West Virginia Code, Article 29, Section 29-19-1 et seq. (1977).

Statute Summary: Every non-exempt organization must file a registration statement with the secretary of state, and refile the statement in each subsequent year that solicitation is conducted within the state.

Exemptions: Churches and other federally tax-exempt religious organizations, accredited educational institutions, non-profit hospitals, membership groups, and organizations that receive less than $7,500 in annual contributions are exempt. However, an application for exemption must first be submitted.

Penalties: Violation of the statute can lead to an investigation, revocation or suspension of registration, or criminal prosecution. The court is also authorized to place the organization's contributions into receivership, for disbursement to donors. The Commission on Charitable Organizations promulgates rules, regulations, and forms, and holds hearings and makes adjudications.

State Contact Person: Director, Charitable Organizations, Office of the Secretary of State, Capitol Building, 1800 Washington Street, Charleston, W. VA 25305, (304) 348-2112.

Organizations Registered: None.

Wisconsin

Applicable Statute: West's Wisconsin Statute Ann., Section 440.41 et seq. (1961).

Statute Summary: Registration statements must be filed with the Department of State. The statement may remain in effect for a prescribed period or on a continuing basis.

Exemption: Exempt organizations include religious agencies, educational institutions that solicit students and alumni, certain local community organizations, and veterans' organizations.

Penalties: Investigation or criminal prosecution are both available.

State Contact Person: Department of Regulation and Licensing, Room 285, 1400 East, Washington Avenue, Madison, Wisconsin 53702, (608) 266-0829.

Organizations Registered: None.

Wyoming—No statute.

Appendix F
An Exchange

The following exchange of correspondence between Capital Legal Foundation and Mr. Alan Morrison, Director of the Public Citizen Litigation Group, creates considerable doubt as to whether or not Mr. Nader has actually severed his ties with Public Citizen, Inc.

CAPITAL LEGAL FOUNDATION

700 E STREET, S.E.
WASHINGTON, D.C. 20003
Tel. (202) 546-5533
Telex: 904022-CAPLEGFD-WSH

President, **Dan M. Burt**

January 25, 1982

Mr. Ralph Nader
Center for the Study of Responsive Law
1530 P Street, N.W.
(Buzzer #5)
Washington, D.C. 20005

Dear Mr. Nader:

We are in the process of publishing a book which the Capital Legal Foundation researched and wrote, entitled <u>Abuse of Trust-A Report on the Nader Network</u>.

By this letter we offer you the opportunity to inspect a "galley" copy of this book at any time within the next thirty days to review its factual accuracy.

We will make a copy of the "galleys" available to you at our offices and will assign you a private room to read this book, should you wish to do so.

Please advise me of your wishes in this matter.

Very truly yours,

Dan M. Burt

DMB/prf
cc: Mr. David Branson
     White and Case
     1747 Pennsylvania Avenue, N.W.
     Suite 500
     Washington,D.C. 20006

Certified Mail -- Return receipt requested

February 8, 1982

Registered Mail - Return Receipt Requested

Mr. Dan M. Burt
President, Capital Legal Foundation
700 E St. S.E.
Washington, D.C.   20003

Dear Mr. Burt:

Your letter of January 25, 1982, addressed to Mr. Nader, concerning your book entitled <u>Abuse of Trust - A Report on the Nader Network</u>, has been referred to me. Your proposal that we review the galleys of the book in a room at your office is wholly unsatisfactory since it would require us to examine the material without access to our own files and under conditions that we consider to be inappropriate for consideration of a volume that - according to its title - is obviously critical of our work. We are unaware of any author who limits access for reviewers in the manner that you have proposed, and it is our intention not to attempt to review your materials under such unreasonable conditions.

As an alternative we suggest that, if you truly desire a review for factual errors, you provide us a copy of the galleys for our review in our offices. We would undertake to review the materials promptly after they are received. In such case, we would be willing to honor any embargoes that you may impose. We are also willing to discuss the matter further with you.

Please advise me promptly of your response.

Sincerely,

Alan B. Morrison

cc: David Branson, Esq.
      White & Case

      Board of Directors
      Capital Legal Foundation

DATE DUE

7-17-86	WITHDRAWN		
ILL 6-17-89			
MR 09 '90			
FE 20 '96			

DEMCO 38-297